Into the Mind of a Young Entrepreneur

Into the Mind of a Young Entrepreneur
Copyright © 2021
Student Press Initiative / Individual Authors
ISBN: 9-781365-240713
All rights reserved. This book or any portion thereof may not be reproduced or used in any manner whatsoever without the express written permission of the publisher except for the use of brief quotations in a book review or scholarly journal.

SPI Educator: Ashlynn Wittchow, Jorge Beltran

Principal: Alice Bajana-Vega

Classroom Teachers: Melody Ramnath, Tasania McPherson, Ariane Torres

Director, SPI: Dr. Cristina Compton
Founding Director, SPI: Erick Gordon
Director and Founder, CPET: Ruth Vinz
Front Cover Design: Karen Fernandez
Full Cover Design: Kapo Amos Ng
Interior Layout: Jorge Beltran & Ashlynn Wittchow
Photographs: Individual Authors
Back Blurb: Valerie Flores

Student Press Initiative (SPI), Box 182
The Center for the Professional Education of Teachers
Teachers College, Columbia University
525 West 120th Street
New York, NY 10027
www.tc.edu/cpet

Foreword

According to Merrian-Webster, a business can be defined as "a usually commercial or mercantile activity engaged in as a means of livelihood." This year, our students at Bronx High School of Business engaged in the process of writing business proposals. In looking at samples of what students submitted, it was no surprise that in the turbulent year that we have had, many students created business proposals that appealed to our humanity and social-emotional well-being.

In creating a successful business, entrepreneurs should ask themselves some very important questions--What makes me happy? How does my product or service enhance people's lives? Is my product or service helping address a societal need? In today's world, we can no longer afford for entrepreneurs to solely think of the wealth they will accumulate for themselves. They must think bigger and think about the impact that they will have on the whole of society. Whether they did so intentionally or not, it is my belief that our students in this collection of business proposals did that. Not only did they create proposals around things that they are passionate about, but they were thoughtful in how their products and services would bring joy and well-being to their communities. It is of great comfort that these are our future leaders and entrepreneurs.

Ms. Alice Bajana-Vega
Principal
Bronx High School of Business

Table of Contents

Foreword 3
Acknowledgements 6
Introduction 7

Second Period Class 9
Cultural Bakery, Julie Blanco 10
Enphani Dance Academy, Enphani Huskey 12
Health and Snacks, Anthony Montero 14
Unity Food, Tristen Nevarez 15
Dalyyz Jewels, Alyssia Ortiz 18
Virtual Pandemic, Marcos Parreno 21
Golden Glow, Isatu Touray 23

Fourth Period Class 26
The Mystery of Animation Film, Anjalie Bissal 27
Mystical Exotic Cosmetics, Migdalia Colon 31
Heavenly Purpose, Tatyana Filmore 34
Vel Studios, Komi Gamli 37
The Game Spot, Marcquese Hinds 39
Erick's Customizable Pullover Hoodies, Erick Limas ... 42
Building the Best, Cory Rhiles 45
Cherikee Dance Studio, Cherikee Smith 47

Sixth Period Class 49
Victory, Korean Language & Acting, Katherin Alberto .. 50
Greissy's Boutique, Greissy Bautista 52
Jump Start, Kieng Bonfield 55
Safety for Kids, Jhowensy Claret 57
Drawing - Ideas - Creative (D.I.C.), Karen Fernandez .. 59
Restaurante James, James Luis Fortuna 62
Business with a Mission, Valerie Hernandez 64
Skater Partner and Building Center, Jeffrey Ramos 66
Reality Overdrive, Charles Rosario Chino 69
Fatou's Wedding Extravaganza, Fatoumata Sacko 71
Nature with Yasmine, Wendkouni Sigue 73
The Volleyball Wristband Company, Juannely Pena Bueno 76
Instinct, Frederick Rodriguez 78
Roosevelt Theo, Juan Tamayo 80

Seventh Period Class 82
Antena Inalambrica, Keislyn Bueno 83
Kiddies' Corner, Danna Caraballo 86
Braidy's Custom Bottles (BC Bottles), Braidy Dennis ... 89

Rabi's Artificial Nail Shop, Rabi Mohammed......... 93
SunnySounds, Jeremiah Guzman Rodriguez......... 96
Blush Boutique / Moon Art, Suponna Nfn......... 99
Diva Gloss (Bossy Beauties), Dennis Pena Ledger......... 102
Vianca's Joyas, Vianca Santana......... 106
Wilson's Bakery, Wilson Segarra......... 108
Fire Drawing Co., Janniyah Strong......... 110
AnimeDezigns, Jeremy Ventura......... 113

Acknowledgements

For the second year in a row, the COVID-19 pandemic introduced unexpected obstacles in the face of remote & blended learning. Our tenacious freshman class did not let this affect their abilities to achieve their goals. The completion of this book has been a long journey, amidst technological issues and emotional challenges in the last leg of the school year. Thankfully, we had a strong community lending their immense support to us all both at home and here at BHSB.

With so many to thank, we would like to thank those who were directly involved in the publication of this book. We begin by saying thank you to the Student Press Initiative at Columbia University's Teachers College who gave us the necessary resources and support for our project. Thank you to Jorge Beltran and Ashlynn Wittchow who took the time to work with us to develop and administer instruction on the useful art of business proposal writing all while remote. We are grateful for their presence and their devotion to this project.

Next, we would like to take the time to thank our teachers who were involved in all aspects of publishing this book as well. Melody Ramnath, Tasania McPherson, and Ariane Torres - our blended and online instructors - provided insightful leadership and knowledge to complete this project successfully. Thank you so much for your continuous support and presence whenever needed.

Additionally, we are grateful to our wonderful BHSB school principal Alice Bajana-Vega and her administrative staff for believing in and funding this program. In addition, much gratitude goes to The Committee for Hispanic Children and Families for their extra financial support. They continue to be an integral part of our community here at BHSB, and for that, we are forever grateful.

Lastly, there's us! The emerging entrepreneurs! We put a lot of work into relaying our passions, articulating our values, utilizing our brain power, and displaying our hard work and dedication through our business proposals. We hope you take away from this that we not only care about our personal futures, but the future of the world around us as well. Thank you for taking the time to read our work.

Now... who are YOU betting on to turn their business dreams into reality?

The Young Entrepreneurs at BHSB
Ninth Grade ELA Students
2020 - 2021 School Year

Introduction

As discussed by Shannon Carlin in her 2016 article, "in the final moments of [Beyoncé's song] "Freedom," an older woman's voice is heard saying: "I had my ups and downs, but I always find the inner strength to pull myself up. I was served lemons, but I made lemonade." This is the voice of Hattie White, Jay Z's grandmother, taken from a speech she gave at her 90th birthday party last April in Clayton, Delaware."

We all might have come across this quote at one point or another, however turning lemons into lemonade sounds all the more possible when coming from a family elder that Beyoncé & Jay Z share. This quote sounded all the more inspirational as we were working to consider different ways we can turn negatives into positives throughout this second year of the COVID-19 global pandemic.

It is safe to say that for all teachers, it is a top priority to ensure that our students are doing well not only academically, but mentally and emotionally as well. This is especially true during these trying times. Students were provided with many opportunities to discuss issues they were struggling with throughout the year. This was a great release for them, however it got us thinking—what are ways in which students can turn this time of reflecting on the past few months into tangible ideas for their future?

As we have seen, so many people were unfortunately let go from their jobs due to the pandemic. In order to obtain a source of income for their families, people used their time to create ideas for businesses and worked to turn those ideas into realities. For some, their businesses have become so lucrative that they will not have to worry about clocking into a 9 to 5 job any time soon. This has proved to be especially true for black and brown people, as small business ownership has surged in these communities during the pandemic.

There are many students in our very own New York City schools that have utilized this time to turn their passions into small businesses. In my network alone, I have seen a number of students monetize their creative abilities. These young entrepreneurs have inspired me to work to do the same! This is where the idea for the emerging entrepreneurship project came from. If we gave all students the time and space to consider what they love to do and the needs they see in their communities, we could potentially end up with 1.1 million small businesses throughout the city!

The collective ninth grade class here at the Bronx High School of Business took their time and used a great deal of mental strength while thinking through different ideas for the emerging entrepreneurship project. They considered potential products and services, sales strategies, ethical business practices, their friends and families, in addition to their local and global communities to complete this project. We hope that students enjoyed squeezing every drop out of their metaphorical lemons to create some juicy, sweet, and refreshing lemonade. We hope to see these amazing business ideas become realities for students in their future as well.

Thank you for picking this book up! We wish you well and hope that it serves to inspire you in both small and large ways. If there is anything you should remember after reading this work, it is to seek out your inner strengths to turn all of life's lemons into lemonade.

Melody Ramnath
ELA Teacher
Bronx High School of Business

Second Period Class

Cultural Bakery
Julie Blanco

Have you ever been out of your country or just started living in a city, but you're craving that special treat from back home? Like tres leches? Then visiting my bakery is what you need. Hi, my name is JB, and I'm the owner of Cultural Bakery. My bakery specializes in desserts from all over the world. Starting with the coffee, you will not be disappointed in the diversity of options you can choose from. One important fact about my bakery is that not only the food is diverse, but also the employees. At Cultural Bakery, we do not discriminate against your background, race, or gender. Also, our secret is to hire employees from different parts of the world to teach us the different goods they have where they live. And yes, all of our food is made from scratch since we want the best for our customers.

What makes my product special is that it's something you can't find anywhere because when opening a bakery, people only like to focus on one thing and start growing their bakery after. In my bakery, we strive to make it unique in every way possible, starting from the employees to the ingredients.

My product is important to me because it's something I've wanted to open since I was a little girl and have been perfecting and changing over the years that passed. This would benefit my community because in a way I feel like we will grow together and enjoy the sharing of different cultures. I came up with the idea of my product since I have not seen one place that sells pastries from all over the world and I would like to change that.

My business' mission is to show the different types of culture and diversity through food. My business can be defined as a safe place where you can eat different types of pastries. My business values diversity. I chose to support this cause because there is not a lot of diversity or culture since people have been really racist towards it and I want to make a change in that. I chose to promote this principle because it's something that should be brought to light and talked about more. Promoting this principle would help make sure my business is ethical because overall if you support my business you will be supporting me, my employees, and people out there that don't have a voice.

My product or service will be sold online and in person because you can buy your product online and pick it up at the store or you can go to the store and choose from there. We would also do shipping. This is the best way to reach my customers because they can either see the product in person or buy it from their couch online. I would put commercials on all social media and banners on the street to start getting people's attention. My product will be advertised on the following social media platforms: Twitter, Insta, Snap, Youtube, etc. I chose these platforms because everyone at least uses one of these platforms. Our social media is used to also promote the company value of non-discrimination. This is done by posting a donation link or website for people that would like to help.

Cultural Bakery invites you to try our diverse options of pastries and drinks from around the world. By supporting Cultural Bakery, you're also supporting the different cultural backgrounds that every country has but don't always come to light.

Enphani Dance Academy
Enphani Huskey

Have you ever wanted to play a sport, but it was too much money & there were no teams nearby? Well, it's great you're here because I want to start a local dance team for young girls and boys at a cheaper cost for the parents, so everyone can enjoy the thing they love to do.
My dance school is going to be for any gender, any age, anyone and the class is only going to cost 20 dollars, which is easy for every parent with a child. It's going to be a place where people can feel confident and feel at home. The important fact is that anyone can come in and take classes no matter what age, what size, what gender, no matter what, and it's less money to pay.

The thing that makes my product special is that everyone else is trying to make you buy everything from their website or something like that for them, but I'm doing this for the kids of the future to give them a chance. My whole project isn't about me, it's about the people. The connection I have with my service is dancing. I've always loved it. It was always my favorite thing to do, and there are many kids out there that feel the same way about dance that I do . I came up with the idea because I was like I want to be a dance teacher, and this is what I want to do when I'm older.

My business' mission is to let people know that you can follow your dreams and become what you want to be because everyone deserves to be able to follow their dreams. My mission outside of the business is just giving people hope. I guess letting people learn their worth and how they can be them and do what they want. The cause I would like to support because of this area is nondiscrimination because I feel like everyone deserves the same respect. I chose to support this cause because people get treated differently based on their skin color or their gender when everyone is human and the same we just all look different in their own way. I chose to promote this principle of nondiscrimination because, like I said, in my business everyone will feel the same and feel equal. Promoting this principle would help make sure my business is ethical because it will be a safe space for everyone and it will make everyone feel good when they come. If you support my cause and how I feel about that stuff then you will also support my business because that's how my business will run.

My business will be placed in the Bronx, New York, somewhere on Hunts Point because Hunts Point is so close to everywhere in the Bronx, and that's where my old dance school was, so it's like my safe place - it helps me because dancing got me through a lot of things and overall it made me a happier person. My product or service will be advertised on the following social media platforms: Instagram, Facebook, Snapchat, and Twitter.

I chose these platforms because they all are active, and everyone has social media and can see it there. Our social media is used to also promote the company value of how fun the dance school will be and how many people joined already. This is done by posting all the videos that were taken during the dance class.

I invite you to not only just come to my business, but by coming to help raise money to kids that need it too. Kids that have a dream but can't do it because there is a low money supply do it. You are supporting the kids, not just my dance classes. Supporting the dance school is supporting my cause, which is to give these kids what they want and let them follow their dreams also.

Author Biography

My name is Enphani. I'm 14 years young. I was born and raised in the Bronx, New York. I still live in the Bronx now. My hobbies are either dancing or playing basketball. What makes me happy? My family and friends- they just always know how to get a smile on my face. My family can be annoying sometimes but I have fun with them.

Health and Snacks
Anthony Montero

Naturally, everyone wants to stay healthy, but our aim is to bring health to the body and mind. My company's "health and snacks" product serves as a healthy and affordable snack. My product is vitamins and calcium while remaining a delicious snack bar.

What makes my product special is that it revolves around a goal of both physical and mental health. There are many snack bars in the world, but the majority of the popular snack bars are the unhealthiest snack bars that are full of too much fat and calories. This is why I want to make a healthy snack bar that can help balance the scale. Because of the pandemic, I haven't been able to go out, so I decided to focus on improving my health more than ever before, and when I went to the store I was looking for something healthy to buy. All the snack bars were full of unhealthy ingredients and packed with a lot of calories, so I decided to make a healthy snack bar.

My business' mission is to donate to those being discriminated against by their looks and gender. This is my business' mission because I think it's morally wrong to discriminate against someone by their looks and gender. My business can be defined as an ethical business focused on health and helping others. My business values helping others stay healthy and well. I chose to support this principle of Fair-Trade cause because I believe it's morally wrong to discriminate against someone by their looks and gender.

My product or service will be sold in stores, shops, malls, and online. This is the best way to reach my customers because making the product easily accessible will promote new customers. My product or service will be advertised on Youtube because a lot of people use it, and when a Youtube ad appears you have 5 seconds to catch the audience's attention until the skip button is accessible. Our social media is used to also promote the company value of nondiscrimination and gender equality. This is done by posting various motivational videos and messages.

Unity Food
Tristen Nevarez

My goal is to spread joy through the goodness of food, traveling to different communities to provide good and healthy meals through food trucks. I know it's hard to find affordable prices for great food, some people spend half their paycheck just to get a good meal which shouldn't be transpiring, but me building up an organization could not only help you but your community of people who also don't get to have good meals without spending more money than they should be.

My food truck business is intended to feed those who can't travel very far to get food or who don't have access to good gourmet meals without paying a pretty penny, so my food trucks would be able to change that, food trucks would offer amazing services which would leave people happy for ordering from one of my food trucks.

My business' mission is to strive to help those who are in need of food trucks for their community, and this is my business' mission because I feel as though everyone deserves to be provided with good service from a caring and nurturing business. Some communities don't have access to a business like that, so me providing food truck services to these communities would help change that and leave a good impact on the community as well.

My business can be defined as places where all types of people from all different walks of life have the ability to food trucks where they can be provided different gourmet meals at a reasonable cost. Drink and beverages would also be provided as well at a reasonable price. My business values a cleansed and safe working environment for my workers and to put smiles on people's faces in several communities where stuff like this is not obtainable.

The cause I would like to support because of this is access to food because there is a lot of world hunger around the world, and my business would venture on to change that so people who may not be able to afford enough meals for their loved ones can afford food at a price they can afford and customer service that would have them leave with a smile on their faces and keep them coming back. I chose to support this cause because food trucks provide amazing recipes and gourmet meals. The best part is the fact that you don't have to wait for someone to serve you. You order your food; the cook makes your food and then you get your food. It's that simple. A good cause that wants to make people smile and make their day or week better by showing love to their communities and for them to know people should look out for one another.

The way I would sell my product is going to all 5 boroughs in New York then eventually branch out around other parts of the world and reach as many people as possible to provide them with the recourse they need. My product would be sold in a truck. This is the best way to reach my customers because their food gets made for them while they're there, and they can choose what they want and ensure that they're satisfied with what they get.

The way I would promote my brand that I feel most accustomed to is by asking people who get something from the food trucks to leave reviews, and if I keep my business at a good pace the reviews should be nothing but good ones which would overall contribute more and more to my business success.

My product or service will be advertised on the following social media platforms: Youtube, Instagram and TikTok. I chose these platforms because I know when you promote your brand/business enough an audience will grow and develop it can be at a fast pace or slow pace depending on how passionate you are about getting your business out there for it to garner attention.

Our social media is used to also promote the company value of ensuring a positive experience with the food trucks and show that I value them and make sure that everyone that would get something from my food trucks would leave with a smile on their face. This is done by posting pictures with some of the customers to show that people are enjoying my business and what I have done for them but also the community.

We invite you to spread the word about my business, come join us by volunteering, leaving good reviews that would help garner more attraction for my business, invest in my business, be supportive and encouraging and remember your supporting a business that could help change the lives of families who need it and better people all through goodness of food.

You're not only supporting a business dedicated to providing low-cost gourmet meals to those who may need it the most, you're also allowing my business to build up communities and bring smiles and happiness to communities who didn't have them before.

Author Biography

My name is Tristen Nevarez. I'm 15 years of age and was brought into the world in Manhattan, New York. I was raised in the Bronx, New York. Some of my hobbies/interests are travelling. It's usually a great time and relaxing, and I enjoy indulging in playing video games and other things in that aspect. I have a lot of siblings, so my family consists of different personalities so it's never boring in my house.

Dalyyz Jewels'
Alyssia Ortiz

Have you been thinking about small ways that you can change the world for the better? If so, you can start with something as small as changing where you buy your clothing from. I have the perfect brand for you - Dalyyz Jewels'! At Dalyyz Jewels' we offer fun and affordable pieces like clothing, jewelry, and artwork that are not only wallet-friendly but also sustainable and eco-friendly. All of our products would be made with recyclable materials that don't add to toxic waste and would not contain any plastics.

What makes my product special is that all of our clothing and art would be made from recycled materials and would not contain harmful chemicals. This is important to my community because with sustainable clothing, it can not only be used to create other things when it's no longer needed, but since it doesn't contain harmful plastics, it would also be recyclable and not add to extra waste. I came up with my idea for my business when we were learning about how much plastic we produce just by our clothing alone, and it was shocking and sad. And when we learned how dangerous and destructive the clothing industry was, I realized that this is a problem that is rooted very deeply in our society, and we have to find a change before we fully destroy our planet

Dalyyz Jewels' mission is to create eco-friendly products and help my community to be more sustainable. This is my business' mission because I want to create cute and sustainable clothing without harming the environment and help people realize how easy it can be to make small changes in your life that bring huge impacts. Dalyyz Jewels' can be defined as an eco-friendly clothing and art business. My business values are to reduce excess/unnecessary waste, to recycle as much as possible, and to have a safe and healthy working environment. The cause I would like to support because of this is the use of sustainable products For example we would have compostable/biodegradable packaging and tags, we would make use of secondhand finds. We would follow the reduce, reuse, recycle, compost protocol. I chose to support this cause because all this helps cut down on excess waste and can also cut down on business costs. Not only that, but when having an eco-friendly business, your products can't be the only thing that lines up with your mission. You also have to bring these causes into every aspect of your company, and for me, I feel like this is the best way to do that. I chose to promote eco-friendly business practices because I realized that there weren't many affordable environmentally safe clothing brands and that the ones that are out there don't attract teens and young adults. So I felt like there needed to be more cute and affordable options for our youth because these people are our future and are the only ones who can truly make a difference. Promoting this principle would help make sure my business is ethical because the more people that see the cause the easier it will be to put these promises in action. Supporting my small business would allow people to dress how they'd like while being sustainable and eco-friendly.

My clothing and art will be sold on both a website and a boutique-type store. This is the best way to reach my customers because when buying clothing some people prefer to shop online, but other people like to buy in stores so having both can draw in more people. Not only that, but it would be a lot easier for people to come into the store to be able to get the full experience of my business.

My product will be advertised on Instagram and Twitter. I chose these platforms because they would help my outreach with people in my area and people that I'm targeting with my product. Since a lot of young people tend to use those social media sites, it would be best for me to promote my product on these platforms. Our social media will be used to also promote the company's value of being eco-friendly. This is done by posting how our products are made, as well as how to reuse them, showing how our packaging would work, posting facts on my product, and explaining what exactly makes it eco-friendly. Not only that but we would post other helpful information on more vague ways to be eco-friendly in people's own life without supporting my business.

My call to action is to provide an eco-friendly environment and not add to excess waste. We invite you to support my business so I can be able to create a wider impact, and we invite you to create changes in your own life that can help our call to action.

Author Biography

My name is Alyssia Ortiz. I am 14 years old, and I was born and raised in The Bronx. I love the show Good Girls, and in my free time I enjoy making jewelry and painting. One of the main things that makes me happy is seeing my family members wearing and embracing the art that I make for them. It makes me feel extremely proud knowing that other people besides me like my art.

Virtual Pandemic
Marcos Parreno

Have you ever experienced not going outside due to a very dangerous virus?
Virtual Pandemic is a video game that is about surviving, and it relates to what we humans experienced throughout 2020. An important fact is that it is going to help kids understand things of how the real struggle of the pandemic is based on everything: money, food, etc. That's why it is about surviving.

My product is special because, since it is online, anyone can play it around the world, so it is not like you have to go to a certain place to get it. The game is related to me because not only do I like video games, it shows a different perspective of COVID-19. I came up with this because a lot of people went crazy and broke throughout the pandemic because they went crazy on shopping for unnecessary things, so I thought what if I make them see what would happen if they keep doing things like that through a game where you can play it in your free time.

My business' mission is to show kids how a virus changed our lives. This is my business' mission because, for kids, video gaming is like one of the best ways to learn or understand something. My business can be defined as a caring company. My business values that people need to learn how to be safe in situations like that. I always wanted to create a video game of my own, and plus I like survivor games. I chose to promote this principle because if kids stay inside their house playing the game it means there's less risk of them getting sick or catching the virus. Promoting this principle would help make sure my business is ethical because it prevents kids from going outside. Supporting me to promote this game will be good because it not only keeps them from the streets, they are also having fun in a good way.

My product will be sold mostly online. This is the best way to reach my customers because all kids do is watch other people play like Twitch. There are a lot of ads they have to watch in order for them to keep watching the person, so I can pay for my game to be there. My product will be advertised on the following social media platforms: Twitch, Youtube, and TikTok. I chose these platforms because those are the apps that most people use nowadays, and it is easier to find out about the game. Our social media is used to also promote the company value of the new life we live in and we have to be safe. This is done by posting things of what would happen if we don't do certain things, and we can see that or experience that through a video game.

We invite you to support us and help kids understand how important the environment we live in is. The best way nowadays is video gaming. Supporting us to promote this can give the money needed to protest about the environment and how we need to stop destroying it. In conclusion, my product is like a simulation of what a virus can do just that inside of a video game.

Author Biography

My name is Marcos. I'm 14, and I was born and raised in Ecuador. Currently, I live in the Bronx, New York. Something I do throughout the day is play video games and think a lot about how I can be a better person. Something that makes me happy is my family being proud of me for having really good grades, like 95 and above in every class. My family is really big, so if something happens, everyone knows right away. They like to party all in the family. I like to sleep or watch Netflix. In the future I'll like to be the most important businessman in the world, like Elon Musk or Bill Gates.

Golden Glow
Isatu Touray

Have you ever felt insecure about your skin? People may always not feel confident or are always insecure, but my skin care products will allow you to use it on your face or body no matter your skin tone or how your skin is. It will make you feel very confident about yourself and even feel very happy once you step outside and let the world see you.

The product that I sell is soap made from scratch from Africans. My business is called Touch Up Skins. My product is a soap that you can use to clear your skin from any black spots or dry skin. I decided to sell this product because I wanted people to feel more confident in themselves. After using this, it will help any type of skin type you are and to show yourself off to others also to feel very confident once you walk out your doors. My product is for any type of skin you have. It's never about discriminating against others because of the type of skin you have. It's about boosting confidence in anyone you know who has low self-esteem. It's about supporting anyone in any type of problems they have and making people feel way better about themselves.

My product is an African black soap that is made from scratch in Africa, and the people that help make the soap are my people. It is to help remove any black dots from your skin and make you feel confident again. It clears your whole body, no matter your skin tone. I decided to sell this product because I wanted people to feel better about themselves and come to my store and just feel confident in talking about how they want to feel better about themselves.

My connection to my product is to show others how to express their beauty and confidence. Also, my product is made from my homeland, so every time I use it or see others using it, I remember that I'm making a change in the world. I once used to never like my skin or beauty, but once I started using my product I started to open up a lot and feel very confident. This is why I want others to feel what I feel now. I came up with the idea of my product because of how I saw my people back home feel once they walked outside. They never used to have confidence in themselves, so I decided to make this soap from scratch to help others feel way better about themselves and show them that once they step foot in my business they will feel like they're at home and will never go back to having low self-esteem.

My business' mission is to make sure that everyone is safe and not discriminated against while working for my business. This is my business' mission because I want people to feel comfortable where they work. Also, I want people to come to work knowing that they have a home there to be free and safe in. My business can be defined as a no discrimination zone. My business values the way people feel about themselves because I want everyone to feel confident in themselves. The cause I would like to support because of this is the safety of the workers. I chose to support this cause because I love when people feel comfortable where they are and always have a home once they step foot at any place they go to. Also, I would love for my workers to be confident and safe where they are.

I chose to promote the good working conditions principle because I want workers to be safe where they work and to be comfortable wherever they are. Also, the safety of my workers is first before anything because I create soap and that can get a little bit messy, but my workers are always my first check-up. Promoting this principle would help make sure my business is ethical because when people are looking to support you, they want good customer service, good working conditions etc. So these are the things I go for to help my business. Also, I want to make everyone feel at home. When supporting my business, you will never be discriminated against. You will always feel confident and love your body once you support my business. Also, I want to make the community a better place for everyone.

My product will be sold in the Bronx, NY in my store, but I also do delivery anywhere in the state. You can also go on Instagram, Facebook and Youtube to find my product and learn more about it. This is the best way to reach my customers because some people may not live close to me to be able to come to my shop, but if I have delivery they can always have access to me and get their soap and start their journey. My product or service will be advertised on the following social media platforms: Instagram and Youtube. I chose Instagram and Youtube because on Instagram I can do giveaways and connect with new people on the app, and many people are using this app, so they won't miss my product. Also, Youtube would promote my business because I can show my subscribers the skin care routine and update daily videos on how my soap will clear your skin. Our social media is used to also promote the company value of promoting other African and Black businesses, allowing everyone to come out of their box and support one another. This is done by posting funds to help many people who are not able to buy products and sticking together as a whole making the world a better place.

We invite you to join Touch Up Skin and support social justice by showing everyone that either black or white, we're all the same. Also, my company supports people who get discriminated against because of their color. Supporting my business will show you what's going on in the world that is not being addressed and will have you wanting to make a difference.

Author Biography

Hey, my name is Isatu Touray, and I was born and raised in New York. I am from Gambia, and my hobbies are cooking and making people feel better about themselves. My family and food makes me happy. My family is really kind-hearted and cares so much about me, which keeps me moving in life. I want to be a therapist in the future and have a very good business.

Fourth Period Class

The Mystery of Animation Film
Anjalie Bissal

Have you ever thought of turning your whole imagination into a reality? Well, Animation Films can provide that for you, like sketching your vision and putting it on screen. We can help your community to come together to let out their ideas and imagination and turn them into a short film that comes to reality.

Animation Films can spread our message around over the world to encourage people to be safe, like our business is always in a good condition, like, we have a strong building, but not only that is safe, we would spread our animated film to encourage people to be healthy in a time like covid and take steps to avoid getting sick and also we can show them things that can give a happy expression on their faces.

Animation Films is a safe business that can provide you with help, like how to get started on creating sketches and putting it on screen. We also hire people who would like to join the excitement of the job and help people make sure they are protected. Also, the more help my business provides, the more it helps children and adults to feel inspired and great with their imagination.

Starting an Animation Films business connects to how I got inspired because everytime I would draw. I would let my ideas out, and sometimes I feel like turning them into real life. When I do start the business, it can inspire the community to feel the same as I did.

I came up with the idea for my service, which is an Animation Film studio to inspire people because it allows many adults and children to feel free to sketch and put their sketches on screen from their imagination. I also came up with the idea because not only are they focusing on the community, it is focusing on the world by helping because if we are in a tough situation like the Covid-19, we can create a short animated film that can encourage people to be safe, calm, and happy, and to get through this.

Animation Films' mission is to help my community and the world to feel safe at all costs, so many adults and children can come in and share their imagination on screen and turn it into a film to make them feel better. This is my business' mission because not only customers are coming in, my workers and I can create an animation film for the whole world to see so they can feel safe like during the pandemic that is happening now. Animation Films can be defined as a work in progress to make the world a better place, and is working towards donating to children and adults. My business values hope and positivity in the community because my business gives opportunities for people to come in and express their ideas and imagination on screen. That will bring them alive and give them hope.

The cause I would like to support because of this is creating short animation films to spread care and safety to the world, like the pandemic we are in. It can let them be calm. The video goes on to show the character taking more positive steps, such as seeking help, eating well and exercising." I chose to support this cause because it gathers information on making animation films even during hard times like the pandemic, we can create short animation videos that can convince the world and our community to keep safe, healthy and happy that everything is alright, and the more people tend to follow the process of keeping safe from advice of the animation video. This will help the public support my business because we are processing good working conditions in our business and the outside world can all be safe and full of positivity.

Animation films are worked by the employees who work together to share ideas on keeping the community safe and how characters in our animation will provide positive steps that will lead to people being less worried and safer and continuing to live their lives. We are doing everything we can to make the world and community safer, and while doing that, we would donate so people can have healthy lives during the pandemic that is happening now, and they don't have to be worried. Also, it is a way where people can come in and create their own sketch, putting it on screen that will come alive.

If more people tend to follow the rules of keeping themselves safe thanks to the advice of the animation film, this will help the public support my business because we are still processing good working conditions in my business so it can be safe for the community to come in and work on their sketches and turn it into a film.

My Animation Films business will be held in Times Square in NYC near the Discovery Museum, where when you are done with the animated sketch and live film, it will be put up and people will see both of them where they can be amazed by it and how it shows them the story of their imaginations. Not only is it spreading out in a museum, our service website is also open for people to check in and see the things we do and how we can provide help if they want to join the activity. This is the best way to reach my customers because the website shows more for what we do and when people go on it before coming in, they will have a full experience because our website also has a place for people to create their own animation online.

My product or service will be advertised on Instagram. I chose this platform because it is a world-wide media platform, and when I post what my service is about like images of sketches and films being made from ideas and imagination, it can allow people to be more engaged with what my service does and when I get more supports, there will be a chance of gaining more connection with the audience and supporting them.

Our social media is used to also promote the company value of helping my community and the world to feel safe at all costs, so many adults and children can come in and share their imagination on screen and turn it into a film to make them feel better even across social media as Instagram because many people can stop scrolling and see how it is providing them help.

This is done by posting short sketches, images, and short animation films of how our finished products look like before and after, and even in a time like Covid-19. We put together both so we can tell the world to be calm, and the cartoon characters will provide futures on how to be safe and how everyone can support one another during hard times like this.

We invite you to help by donating art supplies and any technology to Animation Films so we can use that donation to help kids and adults all over the world with the animation films we create. With those supplies, we can have an increase of children's experiences with them. This allows the technology to sketch and put it on screen to create a film. Please come to our event, where we will launch our very first animation film that will be able to inspire people and convince them not to be worried in a time like the pandemic we are in.

Creating Animation Films, such as sketching and putting them on screen, can help the community to come together to let out their ideas and imagination and turn them into a short film. Animation films can spread all over the world to encourage people to be safe and show them things that can give a happy expression on their faces.

Author Biography

My name is Anjalie Bissal and I am 15-years-old. I was born and raised in Guyana. I now live in New York City, in the Bronx. My interests and hobbies are drawing and doing puzzles. My family always makes me happy, and "I" make myself happy because I am in a good place, and I feel peace with myself. My family is funny, caring, helpful and loyal. I like to draw in my spare time and watch tv. I want to be an FBI agent in the future.

Mystical Exotic Cosmetics
Migdalia Colon

People around the world want to feel confidence and beauty wearing makeup, while also not worrying about harming the environment. Mystical Exotic Cosmetics has the solution: our foundation, Ebvenley. Our foundation not only blends and matches into your skin tone perfectly, but we also support making a change to the environment by donating to charities, which makes our foundation not only natural to you, but to the environment as well.

If you want that foundation that matches your true natural skin tone, our product named Ebvenley comes in different shades for your skin. It's made by Mystical Exotic Cosmetics aka M.E.C., which Is located at our store in Manhattan, NY. This foundation not only suits your face but also benefits your skin. One important fact to know about Mystical Exotic Cosmetics is that we are a business that supports the environment and ecosystem.

What makes our product Ebvenley special is that the healthy ingredients that are in our product aren't made from toxic chemicals. Few of the reasons it's a good healthy product is the ingredients being made from plants and the product being recyclable, meaning it's biodegradable.

What makes my product important to me and my business, are the benefits that my community and the world gets when supporting us. One of the reasons why I like our product, Ebvenley, and hope more people will try it, including celebrities, are the ingredients that it contains and how it was never tested on animals. We also show that promoting our product can help more customers buy from us so we can help the environment.

How I came up with the idea to start Mystical Exotic Cosmetics and my product Ebvenley, was one day I thought, "Why aren't more companies having more diverse skin tones?" and "Why isn't there a healthy option instead of using toxic chemicals?" and "Why are some of them so expensive to buy?" So, then I decided to start my business from there on and decided I wanted to make a change to help not only the community but the world and the environment.

My business' mission is to help the community, and we do that by donating to charities and making our products more affordable. This is my business' mission because we not only want to make people feel beautiful and have more confidence, but we also want to donate to charities like Earthjustice that support the people and the community. My business can be defined as a supportive business that cares if our products are safe to others and is not harmful to the environment.

My business values responsibility because we are responsible to know where our products go after being used and what types of chemicals aren't toxic to use in our ingredients. The cause I would like to support because of this are charities that help the community and environment. Earthjustice is a charity that protects people's health and preserves places and wildlife. Earthjustice is a nonprofit public interest environmental organization that helps the people and the environment. I chose to support this cause because it's a big organization that cares for the earth by taking care of people's needs, the wildlife, and preserving the places. I chose to promote this principle because we give a portion of our earnings to support this charity.
Promoting this principle would help make sure my business is ethical because we also want to be a part of making a change, and that is avoiding any harmful materials and ingredients that can cause to destroy our environment. When we support Earthjustice we know that we are making a good choice, supporting not only the people but the earth as well.

My product or service will be sold in stores and online. This is the best way to reach my customers because we will have employees that respond back to any complaints, and we will have pop up shops for customers to connect with us. My product or service will be advertised on Instagram, Facebook, Youtube, Twitter. We are called Mystical Exotic Cosmetics on these sites. I chose these platforms because they are huge platforms that can reach many different people at the same time. Our social media is used to also promote the company value of responsibility because we are responsible for what goes into our product and where our product's waste is going to. This is done by posting on all of our social media platforms and supporting charities like Earthjustice so you can help out as well.

We invite you to support us because as a business, we are not only selling an environmentally friendly foundation. You are also making a change by being associated with us and that is supporting the environment, people, and also the world.

Author Biography

My name is Migdalia Colon. I am 16 years old. I was born and raised in the Bronx NY and live in the projects. What I like to do is workout. During my free time I like to learn about makeup. When I learn it helps keep me more informed. I would like to own a makeup company that is specified in making foundations that are affordable and safe for the environment.

Heavenly Purpose
Tatyana Filmore

Clothes are one of the many ways where we express ourselves, but the cost of it can end up giving us a negative impact in the long run. My business, Heavenly Purpose, sells everyday Christian-wear with favorable quotes and scriptures that can empower your spirit and uplift your self-esteem.

A mission for Heavenly Purpose that I have is to give back to my community by not only providing a way for the buyer to love and be confident in what they wear, but by also digging deeper to the real problem about changing many of the effects of fast fashion and helping the environment. The idea of my product started with my connection with God. I drew closer and when I started to learn more about him by reading scriptures and stories from the Bible. Through reading, I picked up one of my favorite people, Joseph, because in any bad situation you can make the best out of it. With this story, I want to contribute the same feeling of being inspired by God through my clothes.

My business, Heavenly Purpose with Christian Clothing, can be defined as a trustworthy and determined business. My business values are creating the best experience for the buyer, while also helping the environment, the cause I would like to support. The fair principle trade that I will use is respect for the environment. I chose to promote this principle because of how my business represents all together how we can create a better future for all of us by helping the environment through not polluting with harmful chemicals. Promoting this principle would help make sure my business is ethical because, with you supporting my business, you can stop the effects of what fast fashion is doing to our environment and people, all while creating better self-esteem in wearing the product.

My product will be sold online and in stores. This is the best way to reach my customers because of how people who can't travel to my store can have another way to reach my product online having no issues, while also having the store for locals or just visitors who choose to buy. My product will be available to them at any time.

I chose to advertise on Instagram and Twitter because of how Instagram is an easy way to catch the viewer's attention by posting pictures of my product that will draw the audience to want to buy. On Twitter, I can use the same method to get a click on an ad with the person who is viewing it. Our social media is used to also promote the company value of different takes on how fast fashion has messed up our global society and how we need to change things for the better in return for a cleaner future. This can be done by posting customer testimonials of wearing the product, having pictures of people wearing the product with links to my website online, and hashtags that give important facts about my product.

We invite you to invest in my business by helping make our earth more green and less polluted through making donations of clothing that can be used in shelters. That will be rewarded with a discount on our newest clothing. By bringing your stories to the table and by showing others that what we do now to this earth will affect other generations, we can change that for the better while showing our purpose that God gave us.

Author Biography

My name is Tatyana Filmore. I'm 14 years old. I was born and raised in the Bronx, New York, and I'm still currently living in the Bronx. In my free time I love to read, play video games, and practice on my drawing. One of my interests from being from a religious family is growing my connection with God and learning more about him. I want more people to know about him through the clothes I make, so they always know that he is there by their side.

Vel Studios
Komi Gamli

My company, Vel Studios, believes that video games should be fun and easily accessible for everyone. That's why we're making free games that can be played at a casual or competitive level. We plan to make our games free with multiplayer and optional paid add-ons that anyone can pick up and play.

What makes my product special is the fact that my company makes free games that anyone can play and enjoy. My connection to my product is that I really enjoy video games, and I find them to be a good way to spend time when you're bored. Also, you can meet new people and new friends in online games. I came up with the idea because I was thinking about what product I could make, and no ideas came to me, so I went with something I know a lot about and I'm passionate about, which is video games.

My business' mission is to create an inclusive environment where everyone is paid the same amount for doing the same work. This is my business' mission because most companies, especially game companies, have issues with paying their workers and many of the people who work there are underpaid. Vel Studios can be defined as a business where everyone is treated equally no matter what. My business values equality for all people of all backgrounds. I chose to support this cause because I feel everyone should be treated equally and nobody should be discriminated against. I chose to promote equality for all because everyone should be treated equally, and nobody should be discriminated against. Promoting this principle would help make sure my business is ethical because it will provide a safe workplace for all workers. Supporting my business means supporting equality.

I'll sell my games on the Playstation store, the Microsoft store, and Steam. The best way to reach my customers is to promote my games online with online ads or to have people play the game and record it. The best way to promote my games is to post online ads or get people to play the game and review it. My games will be advertised on Twitch, Youtube, Instagram, and Twitter. I chose these platforms because there are a lot of people interested in video games on these platforms, especially Twitch. Our social media is used to also promote the company value of equality for all. This is done by posting posts that promote anti-discrimination efforts.

We invite you to support Vel Studios and help us bring happiness and joy to people's living rooms. By supporting Vel Studios, you are supporting us on our mission to bring equality to everyone in the workplace.

The Game Spot
Marcquese Hinds

The name of my business is The Game Spot (TGS). "Our goal as a company is to make sure our Audience/Customers are satisfied with our product." Our product is made for people to use when being bored and also for people to be happy and enjoy time with their family. Our company makes all types of games for families and friends to play with each other, but our company is good for the community because it can improve manual dexterity and also teach you to become a better problem solver (scientifically proven).

Our product is games. The thing that makes our product special is the fun you get to have when you buy it. Games from our company are made to have a great time with family and friends. Our games help people get closer and bond together. My product is something that I came up with (games). My product is important to me because I made games for people to enjoy ,laugh, and just have fun, and there's nothing better than having a great time with the ones around you. I came up with my idea after noticing that most games out right now are boring and getting too old, so I decided to create my own and put what I noticed other games forgot to add (bug fixes, glitches).

My mission is for families to have fun and have a great time. This is my business' mission because nowadays it's not easy finding fun games anymore. "Without the proper workplace safety measures in place, a company puts its employees, customers, brand reputation and revenues in danger. Additionally, failure to teach employees how to maintain a safe work environment may lead to on-the-job accidents, injuries and, worst of all, fatalities. I am focused on a safe working environment." The Game Spot can be defined as a business that makes games for people to enjoy. My business values a safe environment for workers and customers. The cause I would like to support because of this is safety. A safe environment should be the number one thing that is checked before going over anyone's head. I chose to support this cause because workers and customers could get hurt if the building is not safe and checked out. I chose to promote this principle because even though customers are getting respected fairly, the same should go for workers. Sending workers in an unsafe environment knowing that it is unsafe is a bad thing to do. Promoting this principle would help make sure my business is ethical because it will let people know that we respect the environment for everyone that is around.

My product would be available online and in the store. This is the best way to reach my customers because customers might have a question about the product so they come to the store, or they can order it online in case they are scared to go outside because of Covid. My product or service will be advertised on Facebook and Instagram. These platforms are very busy with people that want to buy something new every day. Our social media is used to also promote the company value of nondiscrimination and gender equality. This is done by posting on social media.

We invite you to come to our store and support my company, where we create different types of games. I would want my audience to support my company because we are supporting a good cause as a company. "Help us by supporting us to support a good cause which is keeping the working environment safe for both workers and customers."

Author Biography

My name is Marcquese Hinds, and I am 16 years old. I was born and raised in Brooklyn, New York. I currently live in the Bronx. For fun I like to play basketball because that is my favorite sport, and it also makes me happy. Basketball is a way for me to stay fit and have fun at the same time. In the future I want to be a firefighter.

Erick's Customizable Pullover Hoodies
Erick Limas

When was the last time you felt that your clothing represented exactly what was on your mind? Erick's Customizable Pullover Hoodies are helpful for those who have a specific clothing design that needs help to bring to life. All you need to do is submit your design, and we will put it on a hoodie. This will allow you to express yourself the way you want to without having to look endlessly for the thing for you. All it takes is just a bit of thinking. We will be taking your orders online through our website ecph.com (Erick's Customizable Pullover Hoodies). Once the pandemic ends, we will be making pop-up shops around the city.

Our pullover hoodies are customizable. My business is important to me because it allows me to give back to our community by donating a portion of our profit to a charity of the buyer's choice. This is helpful to our community because it helps a lot of people in need. I was in school, and I had to come up with a business idea for an assignment, so after a few days of thinking, I decided to do a clothing business, but to make it unique. I made it so that the buyer could make their design and customize the hoodies.

My business mission is to give back to the community by donating to a variety of charities to make sure we can help all types of people. This is my business mission because there are a lot of people in need that don't get much help, and we want to change that by donating and helping all types of people in need. My business can be defined as a caring business because we like to give back to the community and donate to people in need. My business values the safety of others and giving back to the community.

The causes I would like to support because of this are helping charities and having good working conditions. I chose to support these causes because I want to make sure the people who need help get help and that people are in a safe environment when they work. I chose to promote this principle because there have been a lot of people who have been hurt, injured, and some even killed while working in places with terrible working conditions, and we want to help prevent that. Promoting this principle would help make sure my business is ethical because we make sure that the workers are safe and healthy. Supporting my business means supporting multiple people in need by donating to charities and making sure that more people get safe jobs.

My product will be sold online on our website, ecph.com (Erick's Customizable Pullover Hoodies). This is the best way to reach my customers because the internet is a safe and accessible place to shop, especially during the pandemic when every second spent outside is another second spent risking the chances of contracting covid.

My product or service will be advertised on the following social media platforms: TikTok, Instagram, Youtube, Facebook, and Twitter. I chose these platforms because these are currently the most used social media platforms, and they would reach a lot of people. Our social media is used to also promote the company value of donating to charity by mentioning that the buyer would get to choose which charity they would like to support when they checkout. This is done by posting advertisements on social media platforms.

Erick's Customizable Pullover Hoodies invites you to support people around the world. By supporting us, you support them. By supporting Erick's Customizable Pullover Hoodies, you are supporting charities that help hundreds of people around the world. Not only would you get a hoodie with your design, but you would also help us donate to people in need and help us give people safe jobs with good working conditions.

Author Biography

My name is Erick Limas, and I am 15 years old. I'm Dominican but I was born and raised in Bronx, NY. I like to play video games and watch entertaining videos on the internet during my free time. Having fun, playing video games, and spending time with my family is what makes me happy. Right now, I am unsure of what I want to do in the future, but I am open to opportunities.

Building the Best
Cory Rhiles

Making What I Can! Saving your time so you don't have to!

At Making What I Can, we make anything from waterproof shirts to laptop pants. We will drive to your places, so you don't have to. You just have to pay us. At Making What I Can, we'll sell out to China so they can manufacture more of our products. There are no waterproof shirts around. At Making What I Can, we make a lot of things. We will deliver to your house. You just have to pay.

I've always wanted to invent and make stuff with my imagination. One time in 2014, my brother and I made a pirate ship out of a nerf gun and McDonalds toys. So at Making What I Can, we will make things so you don't have to. I came up with the Idea of Making What I Can from making sub par inventions.

My business' mission is to manufacture and create safe and cleanly waterproof shirts to populations globally for people from any backgrounds that won't be a problem to the skin and in peoples' lands and waters. At Making What I Can we are looking forward to mass producing products that won't lead to short term or long term waste.

We also invite you to obtain our products because at Making What I Can, we also try to save our environment from being trashed. When you purchase our products you are ensuring your part in hindering waste.

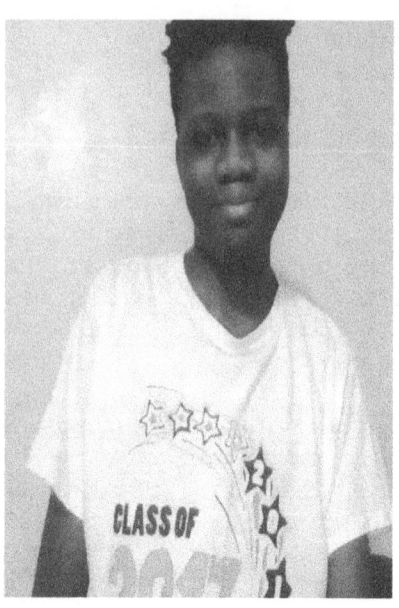

Author Biography

My name is Cory Rhiles. I'm currently 14 years old. I was born on the west side of the Bronx, location hasn't changed. My family is always trying to do the right things. I like taking notes. I like playing video games. I also like exploring the Bronx and most of the parks. Exploring makes me happy. I take notes in my spare time, and I'd like to be a manufacturer in the future.

Cherikee Dance Studio
Cherikee Smith

Welcome to Cherikee's Dance Studio, where safety is our top priority and feeling/looking good is our main goal. Did you know that there are very few studios here in NYC that offer dancing and complimentary jewelry pieces? What makes my studio jewelry so special is that it is real jewelry and it wont turn colors.

A brief important fact about my product or service is making sure it's safe for me. What makes this so great is that people can do something they love and it's safe for people. And you can ask me questions to help improve my dance studio and the jewelry. What can I do better to make you want to stay and come here every day?

What makes my studio special is that we have the best jewelry and on top of that people that like to dance can go to my dance studio. You can wear jewelry anywhere you go or to a party. I would have fancy jewelry. This is important that I came up with a Cherikee Dance Studio because I love dancing and I will like my own name.

The mission for my dance studio is to create a safe place for young people to come and express themselves. My business' mission is to give them fair wages. This is my business' mission because they will get paid. My business can be defined as a business where they get paid a fair amount and it supports good working conditions. My business values fair pay and good working conditions. I chose to support this cause because it is safe for them, and you will get paid a fair amount.

My product or service will be sold on Instagram. This is the best way to reach my customers because they can look at the dance studio and know what is being offered and that it is fun and safe. I would take pictures showing you how it looks. It will represent that it is safe, is it clean and would I like it. My product or service will be advertised on the following social media platforms: Instagram. I chose this platform because I can take good pictures and see if they want to go to my dance studio. It depends on how it looks, making sure it is safe for people and good working conditions and its nice a dance studio. Our social media is used to also promote the company value of safety by making sure it's clean and safe. This is done by posting, making sure it's clean and safe. They need to see how it looks because if it's not clean and not safe they are not going to come so I need to take these pictures.

We invite you to Cherikee Dance Studio. The action I am going to take is making sure that it is safe when they come to my dance studio. I'm

47

going to try to make it clean for them and you will get paid good wages. I will make sure it's safe and clean when they come to my dance studio and they can have fun. They can help by asking questions to make my dance studio better. The goal is making sure that it is safe.

Author Biography

My age is 16. I was born in Manhattan, and I was raised in the Bronx. My interests and hobbies include decorating, listening to music, cooking, and baking. What makes me happy is listening to music. What my family likes is going to events together as a family. In my spare time I enjoy dancing and making videos on Tik Tok. I want to have a career that makes a lot of money.

Sixth Period Class

Victory, Korean Language and Acting
Katherin Alberto

Victory, Korean Language and Acting tiene como objetivo cambiar y ayudar a las personas a que puedan actuar y hablar en el idioma coreano. Esto permitirá que las personas puedan socializar con las personas que hablan el idioma coreano y ayudará a quitar todo tipo de obstáculo en el idioma aprendiéndolo.

Mi servicio se trata de una academia para poder aprender el idioma coreano y dar clases de actuación, ya que muchas personas se interesan en aprender el idioma coreano. A muchas personas les llama la atención Corea y lo difícil es el idioma.

La misión de mi empresa es poder enseñarles, a las personas Interesadas aprender el idioma coreano y no discriminar a las personas que son de diferentes países, o por su color de piel. Esta es la misión de mi negocio porque quiero que muchas personas aprendan que la discriminación no es buena para ninguna persona que nadie, tiene el derecho de juzgar a nadie. Mi negocio se puede definir como emocionante y práctico. Los valores de mi empresa son tener responsabilidad, respetarse mutuamente, honestidad, responsabilidad, amor y alegría. La causa que me gustaría apoyar por esto es No a La discriminación, porque no es algo de que una persona deba estar orgulloso.

Donde son las personas de color de piel diferente y de otros países reciben discriminación diariamente en sus trabajos hasta en las calles. Elegí apoyar esta causa porque quiero evitar que muchas otras personas reciban discriminación.

Elegí promover el principio de "No a la discriminación" porque será mejor evitar la discriminación hacia las personas porque pueden causar muchos más daños. Promover este principio ayudaría a asegurarse de que mi negocio sea ético porque ...no habrá discriminación se trataran. ¡Gracias, tendremos éxito!

Mi servicio se trata de actuación y lenguaje coreano y sería en New York, Manhattan. Mi producto o servicio se venderá en Twitter o Instagram. Esta es la mejor manera de llegar a mis clientes porque sería más extenso y tendría buena calidad. Mi servicio se anunciará en las siguientes plataformas de redes sociales: en Instagram y Twitter. Elegí estas plataformas porque veo que tienen más calidad.

Mi servicio será en New York en Manhattan y se trata de poder actuar y hablar o aprender lo que se trata del idioma coreano.

Nuestras redes sociales también se utilizan para promover el valor empresarial de Mi servicio ya que se anunciara. Esto se hace publicando en Instagram y Twitter, porque veo que tiene más calidad de servicio.

Te invitamos a poder compartir con nosotros y aprender lo que es el Idioma coreano. Te brindamos apoyo, esto es como mi empresa puede ayudarte. Lo que hace mi empresa es poder enseñarte, que no importa de qué lugar tu seas, tú puedes hacer lo que a ti te gusta. Por eso, mi empresa te ayudará.

Author Biography

My name is Katherin Alberto, I am 15 years old, I was born in Honduras, I was raised in the Bronx , New York. I really like Kpop and K-dramas. My favorite hobby is watching K-dramas. It makes me happy to be with my sisters. In my free time, I listen to music. In the future, I want to be a very successful person.

Greissy's Boutique
Greissy Bautista

Have you ever struggled finding good quality clothes that are affordable? I'm here to introduce Greissy's Boutique, offering you affordable clothing for everyday wear. Greissy's Boutique has quality and great prices so that anyone can feel and look their best at all times.

Greissy's Boutique represents me because I want to provide people with good quality clothing that is designed to last long. Our clothing is targeted to ages 15 to 35. Casual, sporty, formal, and lounge wear. Some material clothing will be silk, cotton, leather, and more. They will be fired well and are comfortable.

My inspiration came when I was purchasing clothing from some brands, and they were pricey for really poor quality. Also thought that I was not the only one going through this, so I wanted to be able to have great quality clothing that is fashionable and at an affordable price.

My business' mission is to provide affordable and cute clothing so that people can feel confident. This is my business' mission because everyone should feel good about what they are wearing. My business is providing good quality for my customers and that my employees are being paid fairly. My business values fair payment. The cause I would like to support because there's a lot of people in poverty. I chose to support this cause because, "A decent standard of living—one that covers basic needs and supports an existence worthy of human dignity—is a human right." I chose to promote this principle because people deserve human dignity. Promoting this principle would help make sure my business is ethical because human dignity means to be able to get food, a place to live, healthcare, and to get these things you need a living income. Supporting my business means supporting fair payment for employees and getting good quality clothing.

My product or service will be sold on my online website with worldwide shipping and in store. This is the best way to reach my customers because some people may want to buy it in stores, but others can't go to the store whether that is that there is no store near where they live or can't go so I will provide my customer with another way to shop by making an online app. My product or service will be advertised on the following social media platforms: Tiktok and Instagram. I chose this platform (these platforms) because I can make videos so that people can see it since it is some of the most used platforms right now. Our social media is used to also promote the company value to promote my company value of fair payment. This is done by posting my company mission statement, our wage sheet and our benefits.

We invite you to invest in us because you're not only getting cute, good material, and affordable clothing, you're also supporting the importance of paying workers fairly. Supporting my business means supporting fair payment for employees and getting good quality clothing.

Author Biography

My name is Greissy Bautista and I am 15 years old. I was born in Dominican Republic but raised in the Bronx. I currently live in the Bronx. While I don't have many hobbies, I do enjoy watching movies, babysitting, and watching Tiktok. Something that makes me happy is sleeping, spending time with friends and family. I have a really big family. They are all very funny and loud . In the future I want to be a real estate agent and an investor.

Jump Start
Kieng Bonfield

At "Jump Starter" we help people with starting their business and helping them make money to turn their life around. My product is special because it can help people bring out their true selves and express who they really are. My product is important because I worked hard on it. Also I made it for people when they don't seem like themselves. I wanted to help people express who they really are and don't be afraid of how people see them. I came up with the idea because I see how people treat other people that's different and i didnt like it so my product is to help people from being talked about or bullied.

My business' mission is to make sure I touch the hearts of the people and make sure my product is good for them. This is my business' mission because I like to help people that can help themselves and I want to make people have a smile on their face. My business can be defined as a caring spot for people to enjoy who they are. My business values people and families that use my product. The cause I would like to support because of this is gender equality. I chose to support this cause because I would have all types of people working at my business no matter the gender and I believe in equal pay with both genders. I chose to promote this principle because I believe that all genders should be treated the same. Promoting this principle would help make sure my business is ethical because people would know I believe in gender equality and people would know that any gender can work for me also that my product is for anyone. Remember to live your life how you want and do what makes you happy.

My product or service will be sold by advertising my product. This is the best way to reach my customers because they can see how my stuff works and the benefits it brings and know that they can hit my business up if they want something. I would promote my stuff by showing it to people on the streets and giving samples of it in malls. My product or service will be advertised on the following social media platforms: Instagram, Facebook, and Twitter. I chose these platforms because these platforms have people that support business like me and my product will be able to reach a lot of people. Our social media is used to also promote the company value of people that use our product and show other people how good it is. This is done by posting videos of people using the product.

We invite you to invest in us. By supporting jump starters you are helping people to become successful and helping them get a jump start on their career. By supporting us you will be helping thousands of people with potential become great and you will be turning their life around.

Safety for Kids
Jhowensy Claret

Hey parents, are you guys worried about your kids playing violent games? My product is going to be an online website where parents can download an extension to prevent their kids from playing violent games. It is important to take care of your kids, not only physically but mentally too, because kids like to play violent games. It's like an attraction they have for these games.

What makes my product special is that it is unique and that I'm going to be giving the opportunity and the chance to these parents to control their kid's mental learning. These kids can't be playing these games that contain strong language, use of alcohol, etc. I have a connection with this product because it is going to help me with my future kids, it is going to help other future parents and even the kids themselves. Is also important to the community because kids need to learn good things, and what these kids are learning at home is not good. For example, like how to shoot a gun and other violent things that a teen shouldn't be learning.

I came up with the idea because I play a lot of games too and I thought, "Why not do an extension for parents so kids don't play these violent games?" Thanks to my teachers too that helped me with the idea.

My business' mission is to prevent my workers from getting hurt or getting hacked. Also, to inspire them to create their own business for these kids' safety. This is my business' mission because it protects important information (personal info). My business can be defined as a helping hand for the kids' safety learning through video games. My business's value is good working conditions.

The cause I would like to support because of this is safekids.com. I chose to support this cause because these days sexual predators often stalk children on the internet, taking advantage of their innocence, lack of adult supervision and abusing their trust. This can culminate in children being lured into dangerous personal encounters IRL.

My product will be sold on the internet. I will create a website so my customers can see what I'm trying to do for their kids' future. This is the best way to reach my customers because I think that people are on the internet a lot and this may be more accessible for them due to the current pandemic. My product or service will be advertised on the following social media platforms Facebook, Tik Tok, Instagram

I chose these platforms to promote because I think that these platforms are the most used by people. And also if I post something about my business on any social media the people can read more about my business and that can maybe convince them to work for my business. Our social media is used to also promote the company value of the safety of parents' kids and a mission I want to complete is to help kids with their learning.

I invite you to meet the only website where parents can feel safe about their children's learning through games. I invite you to host events for my business and attend networking events. Kids are seeing too much violence every day while playing these games and we have to end it NOW!!!!!!!!!. Remember to support safetyforkids.com. Also, you can check on my website for more info.

Author Biography

My name Is Jhowensy Claret and I am 14 years old. I was born in the Dominican Republic, But raised in New York. I live in the Bronx. My hobbies are playing video games, playing sports or watching car modifications. What makes me happy is having my dad and mom alive because they are the most important people in my family. My family is nice and caring but sometimes they are serious and strict. In the future I want to be a professional mechanic so I can work for luxury cars.

Drawing - Ideas - Creative (D.I.C.)
Karen Fernandez

Have you ever felt unheard? Have you tried to express yourself, but it didn't come out the right way? Well, D.I.C (Drawings - Ideas - Creative) can have the same idea of this, cuz it's promoting a free world where people can draw.

In the palm of your hands, you will have a product to draw including music and whatever you can imagine to feel comfortable and free to express, create and represent your feeling in just one page, not using words or maybe you can, but more with the power of imagination you will represent an image. My product will be a big opportunity for people who want the same opportunities to draw with the tools they need.

What makes my product special is the fact that it is designed for people who really want to express their feelings through a paper, especially for young artists that do not have the resources to start to draw freely. My connection to the product or service is that when I was young I was unable to draw freely because of the lack of resources at that time, so I think this could help many people to go far away and keep doing what they like with any limitation, just try to dream!.

My business' mission is to help young artists to progress with our tools in this technological world. This is my business' mission because when I was young I wasn't able to learn how to draw with the necessary tools. My business can be defined as a special one because my business is \ trying to help people with this idea. We can make artists grow to make this world more expressive and with more coloring things. My business values are to make this world more expressive with the ideas and collaboration of the people. We can create a game that will make our world more expressive with the idea of freedom. I would like to support this because I think this world doesn't have liberty to express ourselves, so I think that people can try to do it by trying to draw on my platform. Here you will have the tools and everything you can imagine to explore your feelings in just a technological paper.

I chose to support this cause because when I was young I was not able to draw with liberty. And then when I was growing I saw that not all the people in this world are able to express how they really feel in their daily life and the people who do it are judged by others, so that's why we are going to create a game where that type of people can feel at home. I chose to promote this principle because it shows an ethical value to my business. Promoting this principle would help make sure my business is ethical because it's showing that we help the equality between our customers and workers. Let's help this world to be more than it's now, let's make a home, let's play together!.

My product will be only sold online (web) and promoted on Facebook. This is the best way to reach my customers because I'm more familiar with it. I think there are more people who use it, and I don't have a lot of limitations to choose the duration of my videos. My product or service will be advertised on the following social media platforms (facebook, Instagram and Youtube.) I chose this platform (Facebook) because I'm more familiar with it so I think it will be easy to create something to entertain the people and see their reactions. Our social media is used to also promote the company value of making an amazing creative and freedom world as a home to many people. This is done by posting a video showing our game and how it will help us to create this new home for people to be free, to be creative.

We invite you to play this exciting game, to pass time improving yourself with an opportunity to be something big in the future in just the palm of your hand, at home (safe) where now you can have your own office of drawings in just one step, click it and be creative. My business is not just helping young artists, my business is also improving artists that are already with a lot of knowledge in drawing who can go and improve themselves, be creative and spend time with other artists.

Author Biography

My name is Karen Fernandez. I am 15 years old now. I was born in Dominican Republic. I was raised in Santiago, but now I live in NYC. I love to listen to music. My family makes me really happy every day with a lot of crazy things. I love to draw in my spare time. I want to become an artist in the future.

Restaurante James
James Luis Fortuna

El Restaurante James es único por el sazón Dominicanos Ají, Ajo, Cebolla, Cilantro, Sal y Orégano. Mi negocio es único en el vecindario por eso quise ponerlo en el Bronx. Mi negocio vende pescados con fritos, mangus, arroz con habichuela y carnes, sancocho, pasteur en hojas, camarones.

Mi negocio es especial porque por que en mi vecindario no hay ese producto. La PRIMERA forma en que puedo demostrar que mi producto me representa es mi restaurante tienes el sabor Dominicano. La SEGUNDA forma en que puedo demostrar que mi producto me representa es ...poniendo mi nombre en el restaurantes La TERCERA forma en que puedo demostrar que mi producto me representa es ...con la bandera Dominicana. Tuve la idea del restaurante porque estaba pensando y dije que en mi vecindario no hay restaurantes dominicano y por eso elegí el restaurantes.

Mi negocio apoya a los inmigrantes con el pago justo. La misión de mi empresa es que mi negocio se expanda en el país. Esta es la misión de mi negocio que se reproduzca en el mundo porque quiero el pago justo a los inmigrantes. Mi negocio se puede definir como una empresa. Mi valor de mi empresa en pago justo. La causa que me gustaría apoyar por esto es La organización AFL-CIO. La apoyo porque apoyan a los inmigrantes con el pago justo y el bienestar de ellos. Elegí apoyar esta causa porque debido a la pandemia, se han abierto fondos para inmigrantes con el fin que otras organizaciones están entregando para la comunidad migrante ... for the homeless está entregando ayuda en dinero para pagar la renta. restaurantes, entrega de comida) que se hayan visto afectados. Elegí promover este principio porque para que tengan una mejor vida. Promover este principio ayudaría a asegurarse de que mi negocio sea ético porque muchas personas que no están trabajando por alrededor de un mes.

Mi producto se venderá en las redes sociales y también en las tiendas, Ubereats. Esta es la mejor manera de llegar a mis clientes porque es más rápido y se difunde más rápido Mi producto o servicio se anunciará en las siguientes plataformas de redes sociales en Instagram, Twitter, Facebook. Elegí Instagram porque es más popular con los dominicanos y a otras personas más. esta plataforma (estas plataformas) porque se difunde más rápido puedes mostrar los ingredientes. Nuestras redes sociales también se utilizan para promover el valor empresarial de pago justo Esto se hace publicando... unas fotos de tu empresa y escribir un post de cómo es mi restaurante publicar fotos de justicia por el pago justo para promover la compañía y la causa.

Nuestro negocio no es solo un Restaurante también es un llamado a la audiencia apoyar a los inmigrantes entre otros por el pago justo que no le que no le están pagando como debe ser. Te invito apoyar el Restaurante James para que los inmigrantes tengan una mejor vida porque los tratan menos que otros por eso los apoyo.

Restaurante James

Author Biography

Mi nombre es James. Tengo 15 años. Nací en República Dominicana. Me crié allí. Ahora vivo en New York. Mi interés es terminar la escuela. Mi pasatiempo es ver movies, comer con mi familia que es super bien. En mi tiempo libre veo películas. En el futuro me gustaría trabajar.

Business with a Mission
Valerie Hernandez

My business' mission is to helping teens who are abused or think about suicide. This is my business' mission because ... I would like to unite all adolescents around the world so that we can help each other and thus be able to make campaigns to improve our environment. My business can be defined as a place for everyone, without discrimination, fighting for our causes.

My business values design and creating protests and websites where teens can support each other. The cause that I would like to support for this is "we will strike for you, for us, " which is a group of teenagers united by our environment. I chose to support this cause because the environment is important to everyone. Our climate change is getting worse every day. So why not support the young Greta Thunberg who taught millions of teenagers a lesson that makes us understand what is happening with our climate. It is something important that we must fight for. Thirteen-year-old Anna Antoniades, who has been on strike from Penglais School in the nearby town of Aberystwyth, says:

I go on these strikes for my future. Once I understood the real danger our planet was in, I felt like we had to do something straight away. To help us youth, adults need to encourage us to go on these strikes instead of holding us back. Stop telling us just to go back to school. We're striking for what we believe in - and that's saving our world. Why not support young people like me who are praying for something that we should all fight for?

Promoting this principle would help make sure my business is ethical because I would be supporting people like me and promoting my company so that more people know them. Supporting us is supporting your environment and reaching out to all teenagers around the world.

My product or service will be sold online. This is the best way to reach my customers because we will use our voices all over the world. My product or service will be advertised on the following social media platforms on Discord and Instagram. On Instagram we will spread the word and make our business connect in discord, we will work and provide our services. Discord is one of the best places because there are different servers on different topics and where thousands of people can be at the same time, this would be the best way to provide information about our work.

Our social media is used to also promote the value of other companies like mine, that support climate change, non-discrimination and care for our environment. This is done by posting about places where they will make their next meetings link to their servers and information about their work.

We invite you to make our teenagers better people by supporting us, you will make millions of teenagers around the world like your children happy while supporting our community. If you support us, you will also be supporting dreaming children who believe in a better future, that they are our future. it will create better people who believe that our community can be better, that the world can be better.

Skater Partner and Building Center
Jeffrey Ramos

I would like to bring people's attention to Skater Partner and Building Center because my business is a construction center to create more skate parks all over America. It is a project that I would enjoy doing and it will help the community and kids have more places to have fun using bicycles or skateboards. By helping the business, it also helps people that work constructing the skate parks because it creates more jobs. It would also help the city of NY to be cleaner. It means that there are more places than just buildings. Places where people can have fun and a good time.

What makes my business special is the fact that almost no one is doing it so this makes the potential customer focus more on what I'm doing that is unique. I like to skateboard in summer. It is a fun and great thing to do. I was thinking about the fact that New York city needs more places to have fun and a fun thing to do is skateboard so I thought it would be great to create more places that the people can enjoy.

My business' mission is to support families that have lost their job or their source of income. This is my business' mission because I want the business to take more responsibility by helping others. My business can be defined as a help for people that need it and a business safe and with good helping conditions.

My business values the workers that are helping the business grow and get to do more for the community... The cause I would like to support because of this is I Have a Dream Foundation. They work to help low-income youth academically, emotionally and financially over a long-term duration. I chose to support this cause because they have served over 18,000 Dreamers since 1981. The majority of Dreamers come from low-income families, with 94% qualifying for free or reduced lunch. I chose to promote this principle because. They are doing a big job helping dreamers and to keep up the need for money that some people donate. I will help with my business Dreamers foundation so they can help more people.

Skater Partner and Building Center will be sold as a service through my company. And online too so when people click the ad they can go to our website. In the website they are going to show the store location. This is the best way to reach my customers because they may get interested in the business. Skater Partner and Building Center will be advertised on social media platforms. I chose Instagram because it is a social media that a lot of young people use so they can get interested in the business, then I would use Facebook and twitter so adults can support the business. Our social media is used to also promote the company value of care and help to our neighbors and donating to charity. This is done by posting what the business will do and make other people pay and donate to the business so it can keep working.

My company invites you to help us restore Pier 62 Skatepark as we help the next generation of skateboarders master their craft. The skatepark is to make young people have more fun and get interested in skateboarding and also to donate to dreamers' foundation so they can help more people and this will make our community.

Author Biography

My name is Jeffrey Ramos. I am 14 years old. I was Born in New York. But I was raised in Honduras. I like to skateboard. I like to play video games and go to the park in my free time. Also I like to get to know new people and make new friends. In the future I want to work on coding, making and designing new programs.

Reality Overdrive
Charles Rosario Chino

During these times we know it'll be boring to always stay at home. However, what if I were to tell you that you can escape reality while you are safe at home? In Reality Overdrive, lets our users experience the game by letting them use their senses. An important fact about our product is that it has natural resources in which case it will not harm the environment. This will let our users be safe playing indoors while this pandemic is happening.

Something that makes our product specialists would be that we will be the first to try and make people feel as if they are in the game. My connection with the product is that I was the one who came up with the idea since some people would like to get out of reality once in a while or get rid of their problems by playing. I had come up with the idea because people would be bored to always stay in one spot and not do anything. Even at this moment, I'm bored of always staying home.

My business' mission is to make sure that our product will not harm the planet in any way. One way for my product to not harm the environment would be using a battery that can be charged when not using instead of using batteries that will be thrown out once they run out of energy and thrown in the environment. This is my business' mission because our planet's pollution has been increasing due to the burning of fossil fuels.

My business can be defined as a console company where we are trying to upgrade our user's experience. My business values that people shouldn't be bored since all of them are staying inside due to covid. However, when this pandemic ends people could still be playing with their friends on the console when it might be a bad day to go outside or when they don't want to go out.

The cause I would like to support is to try and not harm the environment. I chose to support this cause because since this is our only world so far we would not like to destroy it. Our partnership by keeping the earth clean is our way of promoting the principle of living peaceful lives while taking in the fresh air instead of smelling fossil fuels or gas. Our support of keeping the environment clean and safe will help us live in our world more peacefully and to live beautiful lives.

My product or service will be sold through websites or game companies like Gamestop. This is the best way to reach my customers because since people are staying inside to be safe they can order our product through our website. Or if people wanna take a walk they can visit their nearest Gamestop. My product or service will be advertised on the following social media platforms Youtube because I can put ads between videos as well as making videos on how my product works and explain the product in detail. Our social media is used to also promote the company value of not destroying our only home so far which is the earth. This is done by posting ads or videos on how people can also do stuff while staying indoors.

We invite you to join our community so that all of us not only have a wonderful time playing our console as well as to enjoy yourselves. But as well as to help the environment to become healthier and a refreshing place.

Author Biography

My name is Charles Rosario. I am 15 years old. I was born in Mexico and raised in NYC. Something I like to do is read manga, watch anime, play games, and sleep. Something that makes me happy would be to sleep since the next day it all depends on how you wake up, being in a good mood or a bad mood. My family is quiet but can be bothersome from time to time. In my spare time I read some manga on my table.

Fatou's Wedding Extravaganza
Fatoumata Sacko

Did you know Fatou's Wedding Extravaganza gowns are special? They are handmade in NYC and the product is of good quality. Fatou's Wedding Extravaganza features wedding dresses that are handmade with beautiful one of a kind designs and fabrics by Fatou herself. My dresses are handcrafted here in NYC and they represent my favorite handmade designs and my favorite styles.

My products are special because they represent me. The design is different because they represent my favorite style. I chose wedding dresses because it represents something that I am interested in. I would like to create something different that people will like, especially with different colors. I got this idea because I like when people wear them, so I decided to create my own wedding dresses.

My business' mission is to create wedding dresses and people will feel comfortable wearing them. This is my business' mission because I want to create wedding dresses for people to wear. My business can be defined as a company of good quality. My business values are important because I want people to feel comfortable when they wear my dresses. I chose to support this because I know there are many companies that do not offer quality or comfortable dresses. This is the cause I would like to support because I don't want people to not feel comfortable or not have a good quality of dresses.

I chose to promote the Fair-Trade principle of Respect for the Environment because it is important for our safety and we need to protect the environment. Promoting this principle would help make sure my business is ethical because toxic products that are used at other companies are bad for the environment. I want to let people know that my company is of good quality.

My product will be sold online and in my store. This is the best way to reach my customers because it is easy for them to buy online on my website or in the store. My product will be advertised on the following social media platforms: Youtube, Instagram, Tiktok, and Facebook. I chose these platforms because a lot of people can see my posts and it is easy for them to know where to find my website or my store. Our social media is used to also promote the company value of making good products. This is done by posting about the fabric that we use to create my dresses. Also, posting how we make them in the factory.

Fatou's Wedding Extravaganza invites you to support my business in advance so that we can work to donate $ to educational organisations by offering school supplies and starting a local college fund for a student that is from the community. I remind you that if you support my business you will have fashionable dresses and be in style.

Author Biography

My name is Fatoumata Sacko. I am 15 years old. I was born and raised in Mali, Africa and have been living in the Bronx, New York for a little over 1 year. My interests and hobbies are watching television, doing hair, and spending time with my family. Something that makes me happy is my family, we are really close with one another. My family is very big in Mali, but here in New York, there are only two of us. In my spare time I like shopping and talking with my friends. In the future I want to do something that involves business, but I am not quite sure yet.

Nature with Yasmine
Wendkouni Sigue

When was the last time you enjoyed nature without the internet, phone, or TV to just enjoy the land and nature? These days, my business is important because most of the young people are now occupied by the internet, their phone, or the television and do not take advantage of the area and the nature that we are offered. So, I created these businesses to allow the children and the adults to be able to go out without having to think about their phone or what is happening on the social networks.

What makes my product special is that we spend time connecting with and to know and understand nature. Since I have been in New York, I couldn't go outside, one reason was because of corona, the second reason was because of my siblings, so if I started this business I could have left the house more and allowed other children to go out. I came up with this idea thinking of when I had a babysitter who took us out and we went out to eat and had fun, so it made me want to do it but outside, so that the children can enjoy the area and learn more about nature and the cycles of life

My business' mission is to allow people to benefit from nature and to make more of the real world than the internet-based outside so people can't get fresh air. This is my business' mission because it supports those who have/deal with mental health issues, our outside daycare will aid in providing position experiences and fresh air for those who enjoy nature and respect the environment.

My business can be defined as support those who have/deal with mental health issues. My business values Respect for the Environment. The cause I would like to support because pollution and degradation of our planet is increasing. This can lead to the destruction of our planet, and we only have one planet to survive. I chose to support this cause because I love nature and I want to contribute to clean nature. I chose to promote this principle because of the environment. Promoting this principle would help make sure my business is ethical because I want to help decrease pollution and degradation. To help those who have/deal with mental health issues, our outside daycare will aid in providing position experiences and fresh air for those who enjoy nature and respect the environment.

My service will be offered online and as a Door-to-Door service. This is the best way to reach my customers because a lot of people use social media. My service will be advertised on the following social media platforms Instagram, TikTok, Snapchat, and Twitter. Our social media is used to also promote the company value of respect for the environment. This is done by posting because most of the population, would say everyone uses these platforms so it will be a way to share my service and that many people can see the post of my service.

I invite you to come and spend the day with the patrons here at Nature with Yasmine. My business supports those who have/deal with mental health issues and our outside daycare will aid in providing positions to experienced staff members. We offer opportunities for growth all while indulging in fresh air which is especially great for those who enjoy nature and respect the Environment. Come and join us for a day of fun and exploration, you won't regret it.

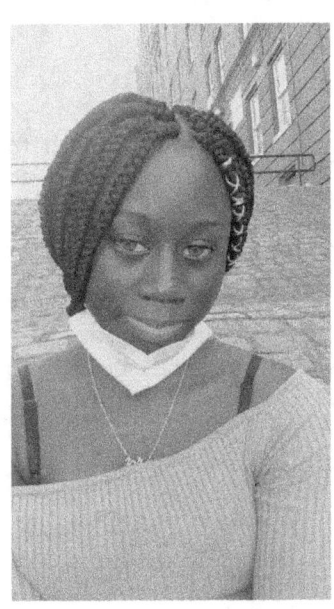

Author Biography

My name is Wendkouni Sigue and I am 14 years old. I was born and raised in BURKINA FASO, Africa. I now live in the Bronx, New York for a little over 1 year. I am interested in science and my hobbies are track, dance, swimming, and cooking. What makes me happy is when I am with my friends and the people I love like my mom. My family likes vacations. I would like to take swimming classes or dance classes . In the future, I would like to become a doctor .

The Volleyball Wristband Company
Juannely Pena Bueno

En la empresa de guantilla, Volleyball Wristband Company, verán que mi inventario es único a cualquier otro ya que hacemos un tipo de guantilla la cual usamos una excelente calidad de tela en comodidad y ajuste para que se ajuste bien en sus manos y muñecas. Mi producto es crear un tipo de guantillas hecha para las mujeres y hombres que juegan volleyball. Ya que será único y los crearemos únicos en gusto y comodidad al 100%, también podrán ver que es excelente calidad. Lo venderemos en cualquier parte del país. El hecho importante es que esto será algo muy impresionante para todos ya que no lo han hecho entonces eso es algo interesante ya que al producir eso la calidad será al 100% lo que será en buena calidad y comodidad.

Mi producto es especial porque me gusta jugar voleibol. Tuve la idea porque antes en mi país solía jugar mucho en un equipo. Porque al jugarlo algunas veces la bola cuando le das un poco duro suele dejar colorados en la mano y algunas veces si le das mal suele torcer los dedos. Para que aquellas personas que juegan voleibol no se lastimen y que se sientan cómodas jugando. Mientras yo jugaba he visto que hay mujeres que se dan duro en la mano entonces mi propósito es que con esto no se lastimen.

El valor de mi empresa será no discriminarnos unos a los otros y pago justo para todos sin importar si es mujer o hombre. Es sumamente horrible ver como discrimina a una persona por ejemplo su color de piel o de donde venga mi misión es hacer lo contrario a eso. Me gustaría hacer la diferencia entre todas aquellas empresas que no tienen estos valores.

Mi producto se venderá en las redes sociales y en una tienda de puerta a puerta. Algunos clientes quizás usan más las redes sociales para pedir sus cosas y a otras personas se les hace más fácil ir a la tienda. Escogí estas redes porque en esa plataforma es más fácil vender mi producto ya que solo usaría fotos y videos promocionando mi producto y sería más llamativo para las personas. El valor de mi empresa es el pago justo y no a la discriminación. Pienso que sería de una forma perfecta promocionarlo en esa plataforma ya que mi empresa tiene como principal valor no discriminarse ya que todos en mi empresa seria uno por que todos trabajan juntos. Lo haría publicando fotos y videos de lo que venderé para que la promoción sea buena y llamativa y también sería buena idea ya que mis valores serían suficientemente buenos para todos y todas en general.

Los llamo para que vean como usaran mi producto y cómo lo fabricamos, para que vean lo que realmente lo hace diferente a todos ya que es único y de todas formas. Esto es un producto de alta calidad y comodidad como les había dicho anteriormente y esto es algo para que vean lo que realmente los hace único he diferente a los demás ya que es unisex, o sea que es para hombres y mujeres en general. Quiero recordarles que esta empresa es única ya que estamos laborando con un tipo de tela suave y cómoda trabajaremos sin discriminación y también habrá pago justo para todos sin ningún tipo de preferencia.

Author Biography

Mi nombre es Juannely Pena Bueno, tengo 16 años de edad. Nací en República Dominicana y me crié en Sabaneta, Santiago Rodriguez, Ahora mismo vivo en EE.UU en el estado del Bronx New York. Paso mi mayor tiempo escuchando música y cuidando a mi primo más pequeño,La mayoría del tiempo me hace feliz pasar todo el tiempo haciendo lo que me gusta y estando con mi familia. Mi familia, ellos son unas personas que a pesar de todos están unidas y te comprenden en todo cuando mas necesitas ayuda ellos están ahí para ayudarte en todo lo que puedan. Ellos la mayor parte de su tiempo cuando pueden les gusta estar todos reunidos en familia también les gusta viajar todos juntos. Quiero estudiar pediatría.

Instinct
Frederick Rodriguez

Have you ever wanted to take your competitive gaming experience to the next level so you can come out on top? Well, our product achieves to drastically increase your precision and your ability to compete to a higher extent. My product, Instinct, is a gaming controller with many customizable options to fit your exact needs for utmost comfortability and performance improvements. We can customize both PlayStation and Xbox controllers alike. My product also reuses plastic in the ocean to create our controllers while keeping quality as a top priority. My product achieves to improve both your gaming experience and the environment alike. We reuse plastic from the oceans to create my products while also keeping quality as a top priority. So you will be able to improve your gaming experience and support the environment simultaneously.

My product is important to me because when I first started getting into gaming at a young age I was hooked. Gaming allowed me to have fun in many ways and escape from reality so I could enjoy myself for a little while. No one enjoys being overwhelmed with some challenges they come across while living their lives. Many people struggle to compete with the equipment that they have so I thought why not make something that can drastically improve your performance and can also provide a quality gaming experience.

My business' mission is to be supportive of the environment. This is my business' mission because I can use eco-friendly materials to create my products. My business can be defined as a gaming product company. My business values keeping quality in the product as a top priority.

The cause I would like to support is the environment. I chose to promote this principle because the environment is struggling from the everyday things we do as a society and the environment is necessary for not only our lives but the lives of all the surrounding living things. Promoting this principle would help make sure my business is ethical because I'm trying to minimize any negative impact that is affecting society or the environment. Supporting my business will prove to be a greater cause for us as a society and the environment so we can further develop.

My product will be sold both, in a store and online. This is the best way to reach my customers because there are many consumers that travel to stores and browse online. My product or service will be advertised on YouTube, Facebook, and Tiktok. I chose these platforms because they have billions of active users. These social media allow access to a larger audience. Our social media is used to also promote the company value of Respect for the environment This is done by posting pictures of large amounts of waste and plastic in the ocean to get users to understand how much they'll support the environment by investing/paying for my product.

We invite you to support our business. By supporting us you will not only have access to a product that improves your overall gaming experience. You're also supporting the environment and the many organisms living within it. We focus on fully supporting the environment while maintaining quality and stability in our product.

Author Biography

My name is Frederick Rodriguez. I am 15 years old. I was born in the Bronx. I was raised in both Dominican Republic and the Bronx. I live in the Bronx. My interest and hobby is playing video games. What makes me happy is playing games with friends.

Roosevelt Theo
Juan Tamayo

Illustrate the future, how it would be if we continue unethical use of company rights, the world would turn into a mayhem, and end the human race as we know it. Cars are a big part of why breathable air becomes unbreathable , that is why we made a better one that helps and defends the environment. My company will at least try to preserve more time than we already do, since cars cause pollution, this creates something known as climate change, which causes lots of ice to melt, causing land animals to die, this also makes the water volume rise and it will end in the land becoming obsolete.

I kinda want to see the world advance more than it is now and I wanna experience, so just my curiosity about the impossible becoming possible. Elon musk inspired, Nikola Tesla also inspires me since he was a genius futurist engineer, he was the one that was able to turn lightning into electricity and making the coil that electrical cars use to be powered.

My business' mission is to save the environment from dying out faster than it is. This is my business' mission because I am curious about the future. Help improve the environment by somehow using alchemy. Well, if the technology is way more advanced than it is now. But cars also require oil, but it is really necessary now because electrical cars have been done before thanks to an inventor known as Nikola Tesla. Although he didn't make cars, he was a man of science, and we can improve upon his technology to make it better than just like we have now.

My business can be defined as an environmental business trying to keep us alive if that is possible. My business values the environment and its state of what it is currently(not good). The cause I would like to support because this is necessary to keep us alive in the next 50 years. This will be for everyone and things that are living.It has been stated by many ecologists that we don't have much time on earth since water level is rising, this can cause the land many worked on to literally be underneath water, why? cause of pollution where's the autocrat to blame lol. Well, it's us to blame for it cars are a major contribution to pollution to which is why i made this company for, electrical cars are superior compared to normal cars since they can go faster and have more features than a regular car does, this helps the environment while also giving you a nice experience in it I chose to promote this principle because in my opinion it's the best if you think about it. Promoting this principle would help make sure my business is ethical because more time equals more things solved. Pollution is needed but we can't have too much of anything.

My service will be sold online but you will have to pick it up at a dealership. This is the best way to reach my customers because that way people will be able to see for themselves even if they don't buy anything. My product or service will be advertised on the following social media platforms: Youtube, Instagram, twitter, and Facebook. I chose this platform (these platforms) because they are the most popular one which means more people will see the downside is there will be competing people resulting in no viewership. Our social media is used to also promote the company value of ...saving the environment. This is done by posting things relating to the environment, like charities and donations for nonprofit organizations.

We invite you to ... support and invest in our company to make change in the world because we want to go worldwide one day but we need what we can get in order to pursue, we won't fail, we will improve. Help us save the environment, the future.

Author Biography

My name is Juan Tamayo. I was born and raised in the Bronx still living there. My Interested in Poetry and Literature and I sometimes practice writing. Although I am quite disastrous at it, I will see improvement if I practice more often. Comedy makes me happy because, well, it's pretty obvious.

Seventh Period Class

Antena Inalambrica
Keislyn Bueno

Ya que hay muchas personas que por la distancia no pueden hablar, mi negocio, Antena Inalámbrica, trata de que compartas un poco más con esa persona. Mi producto diría que es mundial, que probablemente el mundo entero lo utiliza, ya que es un medio de comunicación. Pues un dato importante es que mi producto se necesita en la vida diaria ya que por ahí te puedes comunicar con tu familia, amigos y más. Bueno lo único que yo quiero es construir como una antena para que WHATSAPP tenga señal donde quiera y se pueda hablar mejor. No es que sea especial pero si importante porque por "WHATSAPP" hablamos con personas que extrañamos o que están lejos de nosotros.

La misión de mi empresa es ayudar a las personas con discapacidad ya sea cáncer u otra enfermedad. La misión de mi negocio es ayudar a esas personas que merecen ese dinero o más bien esa ayuda. Se sentirían muy felices ya que al tener esa enfermedad no pueden hacer las cosas que hacían antes.

En este mundo existen personas que rechazan a los demás, si de repente le llega una enfermedad o tienen un accidente y se queda sin un brazo o sin una pierna. El valor de mi empresa es la no discriminación. Diría que la no discriminación es necesaria en la vida ya que si no hay discriminación por cualquier cosa, las personas se sentirían libres de hacer lo que quieran sin pensar que alguien hablara mal de ella. La causa que me gustaría apoyar por esto es St. Jude Children's Research Hospital. Elegí apoyar esta causa porque ningún niño debe morir ya que está comenzando a vivir. Además, el sistema médico de muchos países discrimina a personas por no tener dinero para salvar a los niños con cáncer, pero St. Jude ayuda a esas personas con los tratamientos etc.

Elegí promover el principio de no discriminación porque es un principio que ayudaría a asegurarse de que mi negocio sea ético, porque estoy ayudando a familias que tienen niños con cáncer y a las personas les va a llamar la atención ya que no todo el mundo hace ese tipo de cosas. En verdad si me gustaría ayudar a esos niños con cáncer porque aún son niños que están comenzando a ver la vida diferente mientras van creciendo .

Antena Inalámbrica se venderá online Esta es la mejor manera de llegar a mis clientes porque lo puede hacer desde su casa tranquilamente. Además se venderá en santo domingo en fouce comunicaciones, Antena Inalámbrica se anunciará en las siguientes plataformas de redes sociales en Instagram. Elegí esta plataforma porque tiene más calidad y mayormente las personas están más tiempo en ese lugar. Nuestras redes sociales también se utilizan para promover el valor empresarial de la no discriminación. Esto se hace publicando fotos de mi producto y a quien voy a ayudar si tengo buena venta con el producto.

Te invitamos a apoyar Antena Inalámbrica ya que no solo me apoyas a mí, también estás ayudando a que puedan hablar perfectamente con sus familias , amigos etc. sin ninguna falla y más cómodo y si no que ayudaremos a muchos niños con cáncer que no pueden morir tan pronto.

Author Biography

Mi nombre es Keislyn. Tengo 17 años de edad. Nací en República Dominicana. Me crié en Santo Domingo. Ahora mismo vivo en Estados Unidos. Mi interés ahora mismo es aprender inglés. Mi pasatiempo es ver películas, series etc. Estar con mi familia es todo lo que me hace feliz. Mi familia son personas divertidas, son muy felices. En mi tiempo libre escucho música y en mi futuro me gustaría ser odontóloga .

Kiddies' Corner
Danna Caraballo

Kiddies Corner wants to help those families in need and with no resources to bring joy to their children at home. My company offers children's toys to families for an affordable price. And on the weekends I go to different communities and donate the toys I got left over from the past week. Kiddies Corner encourages parents to donate the plastic toys they are thinking about throwing away, so it won't affect our environment.

Kiddies Corner is a company who sells toys for a really low price, our highest price could be $7 dollars. My company not only sells toys but also donates them. This project/business is important to me because I love kids and I love to see them smile. When kids are playing and interacting with each other, they are the happiest and it would really hurt me if a kid is sad because he/she has nothing to play with. This idea of selling/donating toys came to my mind when I was babysitting my nephew and one of his friends came to play with him. His friend saw all the toys he had and got so happy, but he also said "I wish I had all these toys in my house, but mommy can't afford them" that made me feel some type of way, because no kid should feel like that.

Kiddies Corner's mission is to make kids happy and families less worried about having to buy expensive toys. This is my business' mission because there's families out there who don't have a lot of money or the resources to buy kids the toys they love the most. No kid should be or feel sad because they don't have the toys they want.

My business can be defined as an ethical business. My business values donating to low-income communities. I chose to support this cause because one day my nephew's friend came over to play with him and when he saw all my nephew's toys he got so excited, but he also got sad because he couldn't have all those toys due to his mother's economy. So, this encouraged me to do something for those kids and families who don't have a lot of opportunities.

My company promotes Fair Payment because not many families have the money to buy expensive toys for their kids and some of them are single mothers who have to pay everything by themselves. If you're a parent with low income or no resources at all, come to KIDDIES CORNER, I promise you'll make your kids happy and your pockets too!

My toys will be sold through my website and my home office. This is the best way to reach my customers because some of them don't have the time to come shop due to their job so offering this alternative seems to be the best option, for now. My product will be advertised on Facebook. I chose this platform because a lot of parents use this app a lot. Our social media is used to also promote the company's value of Fair payment. This is done by posting the comparison of other companies' prices with my prices.

We invite you to bring smiles to your house and have a happy kid at home. Come buy at Kiddies Corner, with this purchase you'll not only make your kid happy but your pockets too.

Author Biography

My name is Danna Caraballo, I am 15 years old. I was born and raised in Colombian but at the age of 11 my mother and I moved to the USA because she wants to provide me with a better future. I live in the Bronx, New York. My family is very united, we have our ups and downs but if one of us needs the other we will be there for them. I don't have any hobbies at the moment, but I am concentrating on getting all the credits I can get in my classes because I want to graduate early. I'm still not sure what I want to be when I grow up but I do have in mind studying medicine.

Braidy's Custom Bottles (BC Bottles)
Braidy Dennis

As most people already know, one of the ways we can save this dying planet is by reducing the amount of plastic we are both producing and throwing into the sea. One of the ways we can do this is by telling people to get their reusable water bottles. However, at times these water bottles can be dull and have repetitive designs. And that's where we come in!

With our water bottles, not only are they eco-friendly and reusable. These water bottles can be made to YOUR liking. You can customize these Bottles, choose the size and you can even choose if it's for regular use or athletic use. We want YOU to work with us to not only satisfy you but help this planet. THAT is the goal of Braidys Custom Bottles. At Braidy's Custom Bottles we use Ceramic as the material for our bottles. Ceramic lasts longer than both wood and plastic and not just that, but farming doesn't hurt the ecosystem in any way possible.

With Braidy's Custom bottles comes two main goals. One of those goals is to get the creativity out of others. Our other goal is to help the already dying earth by reducing the amount of plastic. What makes this product different from others is how we work with YOU, our clients, to make sure you can have a water bottle you can cherish. And while you're at it you're helping the environment.

One of the main problems where I live, which is New York City, is the amount of plastic that is in the streets and this plastic ends up in the ocean or an already overpopulated landfill. So seeing that made me come up with the idea that people should not only use reusable bottles but they don't have to use a preset bottle and they can be creative with THEIR water bottle. Not only would these water bottles help reduce the plastic in my community but other communities as well.

I came up with the idea to make custom water bottles because I realized the earth is dying and one way we can prolong the amount of time we have on this planet is by reducing the amount of plastic going into the ocean. The problem I had was coming up with an idea that wouldn't make this any bottle you can buy. I used the fact that most water bottles have the same design and Wondered How other people would like the idea of making their water bottle.

My business mission is to help the environment by reducing the number of plastic bottles being thrown into the ocean. I made this my business's mission because earth is starting to slowly become

Uninhabitable to other species which in turn affects us. because of the way we are throwing so much plastic into the ocean. One of the main things made of plastic we tend to waste are water bottles. The simple solution to this problem is to use eco-friendly water bottles we can reuse. However, if we want people to start using eco-friendly bottles we want them to be intrigued by the water bottles they make.

I would define my water bottle business as a step towards environmental relief. I believe that this business values the environment. One of the primary missions of making this business is so that we can have people cutting down on plastic bottles which is one of the main factors of plastic getting into the ocean.

I chose to support ceramic because based on research from ttps://cedarspringswater.ca/ and Research from other sources, ceramic is made of many minerals and using them to make water bottles is probably the best choice because ceramic is eco friendly and durable I chose to promote the environment because the mission of my business is using materials that are eco-friendly while making sure others aren't using one of the most harmful things to earth plastic. Promoting this principle would help make sure my business is ethical because we're making sure that in no way are we harming the environment while making our products.

Supporting and buying these bottles are just the first step to helping keep the earth healthy. Once you get these custom bottles customized by YOU. You will help the environment since you are reducing the amount of plastic you are using in your daily life. Think about it like this: we did the hard part, and you finish the rest of the effort to reduce plastic.

My Custom Bottles will only be sold online until we find ways to make our custom bottles store. The reason being is since we can't. Make your bottles while you are in a regular store like Target or Walmart. We want to make sure you can make your bottle although you can be premade ones. My product or service will be advertised on the following social media platforms TikTok, Instagram. I chose this platform because not only do these two apps have the largest group of people on them, but Instagram is the easiest app to post ads and even cool water bottle designs made by others. Tiktok also has a big following where we could get tik tokers to sponsor our bottles. Our social media is used to promote our business by telling others our missions. I think if people find out about the way our mission.

This is done by posting how bad plastic is for the environment and then showing them the different ways to cut down on it. One of those ways would be buying your bottle. We would then tell the audience why our product is better than other reusable bottles.

We invite you to create a Braidy bottle because not only can you make a water bottle you will cherish, but you would also be helping out the environment. Remember that Braidy Bottles were made so that you could contribute to helping the environment that desperately needs our help. We can help it by cutting down on plastic bottles which hurt marine life, to do that we need to start reusing things and who wouldn't want to help by using something you created.

Author Biography

My name is Braidy Dennis and I was born and raised in the Bronx. I like playing football video games. Seeing my baby sister after a long day makes me happy. In the future I want to play in the NFL.

Rabi's Artificial Nail Shop
Rabi Mohammed

Have you ever tried an original artificial nail? When you tried it, how was it? Well, I'm here to introduce my product "Rabi's Artificial Nail Shop!" We offer artificial nails that are designed with quality in mind. My product is made with original materials which are good and harmless.

My nails are made with quality materials, and I've made it in such a special way that is far better than other nails. I believe artificial nails are beautiful and unique, and with this, I can incorporate traditional henna designs onto the nails and by packaging my nails in a different and more eco-friendly way. Even though my culture doesn't allow me to put on artificial nails, I want other people to get interested in putting on artificial nails that are safe and they are made with plastic which is harmless .. This idea is very important to me because I think many people are complaining about other artificial nails that are not good, some of them even include harmful products. I am here to make that complaint go away and change their experience.

My business' mission is good working conditions. I will make sure that I provide safe places for my employees to work and have good food. Everyone loves a good meal so why not incorporate this into the business and make it as healthy and nutritious as I possibly can. This is my business' mission because I learnt some of the employees of other businesses don't get a safe place to work and proper food to eat so they end up getting sick. This can lead to the collapse of the business, both physically and financially.

Rabi's Artificial Nail Shop can be defined as affordable but with great quality. My business value is to make sure I use quality materials in making my nails. I want people to know how great the quality of my product is. I chose to promote this principle because I want my customers and employees to be safe and careful when using my product. Promoting this principle would help make sure my business is ethical because my customers will see and know that my products are made with top quality materials. This would further help my business grow as I will get a lot of customers to buy my product, which will grow my business very big and gain more profits.

My product will be sold online and at other local businesses that agree to do business with me and carry my products. This is the best way to reach my customers because I will have an employee working in customer service, so that my consumers don't have any difficulties when buying my product. It is their choice whether to buy it online or from nearby local businesses.

Rabi's Artificial Nail Shop will be advertised on Twitter, Snapchat and Instagram. I chose these platforms because they are places where many people usually go, and I can advertise on these websites. Our social media is also used to promote the company value of good working conditions. This is done by posting videos or short clips about how my employees are making my product and the conditions that they are working in.

Rabi's Artificial Nail Shop invites you to support our company's mission of helping underprivileged youth. We donate 20% of every purchase to a chosen orphanage so that we can help kids get a better life. We want to remind our customers that Rabi's Artificial Nail Shop treats consumers very well and we provide a safe place for our employees. We make them feel comfortable so that they can work well and we make sure that our employees use the right and safe materials for our products.

Author Biography

My name is Rabi Mohammed. I am 16 years old. I was born in New York, Bronx but I was raised in Ghana, Kumasi. I live in the Bronx now. My hobby is to play football with my cousin after I am done with my homework. I become very happy when I am having a conversation with my friends. My family is very kind and friendly. I like to read story books when I am free from work. I want to become a medical doctor in future.

SunnySounds
Jeremiah Guzman Rodriguez

Do you love the planet you live on? Well, I'm sorry but our earth is slowly dying! My product, a solar powered keyboard, will help prevent this because we aren't using materials that harm the earth. Us at SunnySounds are using something you feel and see every day. The sun! With my product we use solar energy to save the earth and bring entertainment to everyone.

What makes my keyboard special is our goal is to help the earth by switching to a healthier, more helpful resource, The sun. I've always enjoyed making music as well as playing it, but I couldn't take it outside because I need to plug it in! So I wanted to help others to do so, along with the earth. I want to make sure my product is healthy for the earth and helps people have fun!

Sunnysounds mission is to respect the environment by using recyclable materials. This is my business' mission because we are able to save and possibly help clean the environment by making sure we take care of it now, so over time we can clean out the past damage.

SunnySounds can be defined as a respectable business because we are tackling a big problem that won't only affect us but all of humanity if we don't start taking care of the planet now. My business values material first in making sure it's 100% recyclable and can be used for other purposes. The cause I would like to support is to take care of how we are making products and the damage it's doing to the earth, we won't be able to live here much longer. I chose to support this cause because we live on this earth and with the way it's being treated right now we won't be able to live on it much longer. I chose to promote this principle because we aren't taking care of the earth well enough to keep it inhabitable. Promoting this principle would help make sure my business is ethical because we are taking care of the earth and keeping it inhabitable and clean.

My product will be sold online, and at retail stores (Target, Walmart, etc.) This is the best way to reach my customers because lots of people go to these places and they may see my keyboard on the shelves and want to try it out. Going online would be simple because people like you could get an ad of my product and may wanna get it as a gift. you may wanna give someone.

My product or service will be advertised on social media platforms because they are commonly used, and whenever someone would search up a musical instrument, my solar powered keyboard would come up as a search result. I chose these platforms because a lot of people use these platforms, and they could come across my product and buy it and they may recommend it to a friend hence growing my company. Our social media is used to also promote the company value of Protecting/Respecting the environment. This is done by posting tweets from actual users saying how healthy this is for the environment. Or we could have our own tweets saying how we make our product safe for not only people to use but for the planet too. We may also show how our products are made to show we keep our word in keeping the environment clean.

SunnySounds invites you to fund us! You won't just be funding a product that entertains you and others. You would also be saving the earth! Purchasing a product from SunnySounds, not only helps you enjoy a fun sunny day, but it also helps the earth recover!

Author Biography

My Name Is Jeremiah Guzman, I was born and raised in the south Bronx and I still live here. Some hobbies I have are trying to learn different instruments, such as right now I'm going to try learning to play the guitar! Something that makes me happy is hearing the notes to a song come together to make that song.

Blush Boutique / Moon Art
Suponna Nfn

Do you ever wonder why mmm does this clothing look good on me? Is it really my style? We always have those moments when we want to feel special. How about a style that will make us feel like that every day? So when I was thinking about a business idea I thought about clothing business and there would be the staff members who'll help you pick a style that you'll love and feel special about, even if it's just for one day. My Company's Mission has always been to transcend fashion, to build confidence and to give every woman the meaning to style her own life. To make shopping pleasant yet inexpensive and unique for women while providing their lives with a sense of confidence and beauty.

In my Blush Boutique there will be 4 categories and the products are party dresses, t-shirts, perfumes and shoes. My business will give away the old dresses and shoes to the people in need.

What makes my products special is it will make people smile and make them feel confident about themselves. My products are important to me because it kind of represents who I am and it's important to my community because it kind of has something that everyone likes, it's also important to the people in general because it demonstrates their mood and level of confidence and domineering. How I came up with the Idea is I was thinking about something that I like and everyone else will like it too and that's when the clothing idea came in my head.

My business' mission is to make people comfortable with a style that they would like to try and always feel special when they wear it. This is my business' mission because there's a lot of people who doesn't like the things they wear and want to wear something different but they doesn't know what style they would look good in and feel beautiful about it so my stuff members will help them pick something they would like all they have to do is ask like "hey could you please help me pick a style?" and they will be in your service.

My business can be defined as a clothing store that helps you find the a style that you will feel marvelous in *I mean that is if they need any help like that because not all the people needs help in finding a style it's just for someone who want to try something new but needs help*

My business values are they all have to be fair and honest with each other. The cause I would like to support because of this is fairness and thinking about others leads to higher personal well-being and everyone should be treated the same and feel respected. I chose to support this cause because it should be important to a person to act with fairness. Supporting my business means you're also supporting the people in need.

My products will be sold both online and in store. This is the best way to reach my customers because it's easier to help them but it's easier if they come into the store. My products will be advertised on Facebook and Instagram. I chose this platform (these platforms) because Facebook the advertisement allows you to target a specific audience. Facebook claims that they are 89% accurate when it comes to targeted campaigns. And I would also use Instagram because the ads are great tools to convert potential consumers to repeat ones your consumers can tag you, and also sell your products on Instagram.

Our social media is used to also promote the company value of facebook and Instagram are used to promote the company value of our delivery systems to show our ads to people who are likely to maximize the amount of value they'll generate. This is done by posting pictures and videos.

Author Biography

My name is Sama Ahmed Suponna, due to a little mistake on my passport paperwork they put Nfn in my name, which stands for no first name. I know it's weird. I was born in Bangladesh in 2006. I am 14 years old and raised in the Bronx since I was 8. Some things I like to do are drawing and reading manga. I like to do those things probably because of my middle sister. She used to draw a lot and read, so I probably got it from her.

Diva Gloss (Bossy Beauties)
Dennis Pena Ledger

Have you ever felt your lips dry and that your lips need more brightness and color? Ok then I got you, I got what you need. You need lipstick that can give you everything you want for your lips, color, brightness, and shine... you need something that makes you highlight your beauty... you need lips diva gloss. Lips diva gloss will give you more shine to your beauty, because you need to shine bright like a diamond. YOU NEED DIVA GLOSS.

My business is about products of beauty like lipstick, to highlight the beauty of women, our company makes lipstick to sell in makeup stores. We got the best lipstick with the best products; we take care that our lipstick is done with the best products. WE TAKE CARE OF YOUR HEALTH. An important fact about my business is that our main goal is your health. We make sure that our lipstick is made with the best product and that none of our lipstick can cause you an allergy.

What makes my product special is that it can help women to feel attractive and to love themselves. The reason why I created lipstick for women is because I want them to feel powerful and beautiful. My connection with my product is that I love how lipstick looks in women. And I'm pretty sure that women using lipstick feel like a beautiful goddess. I came up with the idea for my product for women to give more color and brightness to the Lives of women, my product is done specially for women.

At (Lip) Diva Gloss, our MISSION IS to be sure that our employees have a fair payment because every person who works deserves to have a fair payment for doing a great job at their work also because they are working to gain money.

My business mission is to make the best paintings for home, with the best paintings' ideas. My mission is to create the best animated pictures like paintings, drawing animated paintings to make your house more pretty and decorated, and give your house a more lively look. This is my business' mission because all moms wanna see their house lively and very cute, and the best thing to give your house a more lively look is decorating your walls with paintings, so that's why my mission is to create animated pictures. I want all the moms to decorate their home to their liking.

My values are that we take care of our audience, and we give to our audience the best quality in our paintings, and when i say that we take care of our audience i mean that we make sure that the paintings to make the pictures won't cause harm to our kids. I define my business as the best option for moms to decorate the walls of their kids to give their kids a more cheerful look in their rooms. My business values are to make sure that our employees have a fair payment and respect for the environment.

My fair-trade principle for my business is to have a fair payment. Every employee in my business will have a fair payment and I will promote this because I want the employees to do a great job in my business and also because I want to support this cause so that workers have a fair payment at work. I chose to promote this principle because... because I want to be fair to people who are hardworking because I know that people work to cover their expenses, the work in my business is easy to do but we promote fair payment and support it. That's the main cause. Promoting this principle would help make sure my business is ethical because ... because we are showing to our audience that we are making something great like supporting people who are hardworking and we pay workers devoutly for their work. Supporting my business means supporting my cause because when you purchase a painting from my business you are giving to the employees work to do and the profits will be better for the employees.

Our mission is to sell our painting (frame) online for social media and also in our store located in the Bronx, our sales reach Pennsylvania. If you buy our product online we take it to your home, but you also have the option of coming and buying it at our store and see the option we have prepared for you.

My product will be sold online and in our store, we will use a truck to take your order to your house, we will use a truck because this will ensure that your order arrives safely at your home. So we are going to be using the app Instagram where we will post photos and videos of our products and people have the option to place their order by that same route just clicking a link that will take them to our official website. This is the best way to reach my customers because nowadays people are buying more in online stores, on Instagram there are millions of users and many people who buy that way.

I will be using social media like Instagram and Tik tok. I will be posting pictures and reels of my product on Instagram and on tik tok I will be posting short videos about how we prepare our products and where you can find out about our products and our store. I chose this platform because there are many users on these platforms. Nowadays, Instagram and tik tok are the most used apps.

We will be located in the Bronx and we will promote our product on Instagram and tik tok. Our company value is a fair payment, so we will be promoting this value in our social media, and we will be supporting this value that all employees deserve to have a fair payment. This is done by posting videos talking about our value and the reason why we got this value in our company.

We invite you to buy in (Lip) Diva Gloss, our company, because when you buy our product you're not only buying a beautiful painting you are also supporting our employees by having a fair payment, we support all employees to have a fair payment in their work, So we invite you to support our business because in that way you can support our employees. You can support our cause just by buying our products, you will support our employees, for us it is important that our employees have a fair payment. Because you like an employee in a company you would like to have a great payment.

Author Biography

My name is Dennis Peña. I am 15 year old. I was born in Dominican Republic. I was raised in the Dominican Republic too but when I was 13 year old I came to the Bronx, New York. My favorite hobbies are sports like volleyball and during my free time I like to watch tv shows that makes me happy because when I'm watching tv shows that makes me feel at peace and that's what I like the most "peace". In the future I want to become a lawyer because the law is my passion.

Vianca's Joyas
Vianca Santana

Vianca Joyas is here to help the environment and people's fashion statements, so I combined both in order to help us live a long healthy life and look good while doing it. "Vianca's Joyas" is a jewelry company that makes customizable eco-friendly jewelry for our customers. Not only can you help save the earth, you can wear beautiful jewelry to your specific liking while you're at it. I grew up recycling random wasted objects around my house and turning them into jewelry, so I wanted to share the fun of looking fashionable and living in a healthy environment at the same time.

My business' mission is to help the environment by decreasing chemical and metal waste with my product. This is my business' mission because I want to help the environment and help kids grow up in a healthy world. My business can be defined as a green supportive company that values environmentally friendly products. The causes I would like to support because of this are earth day, recycling, "save the turtles", and wildlife health. I chose to support these causes because according to Gatsby Jewellery,"Often, these harmful chemicals are dumped in rivers, clogging the flow of water and poisoning wildlife." I chose to promote this principle because eco-friendly jewelry lowers chemical waste being poured into water systems and poisoning wildlife, as well as decreasing mining for diamonds and golds, which has a bad effect on the earth. Promoting this principle would help make sure my business is ethical because supporting Viancas Joyas means being one step closer to having a healthier environment. You can look fashionable and save the world while you're at it.

My product will be sold online. This is the best way to reach my customers because it is a safe way to interact with my customers considering the pandemic. My product will be advertised on TikTok. I chose this platform because I know how to work my way around it easier, it's a faster way of connecting with my customers, it targets a lot of people in my age group, and tiktok will recommend it to people who are interested which will help my company grow. Our social media is used to also promote the company value of respect for the environment. This is done by posting what products I'm using and how they are safe for the environment. Also, by discussing the ways my company benefits our environment.

We invite you to the Viancas Joyas family. By being a part of and supporting this family you can look fashionable in your specific taste. And that's not even the best part, by supporting our company you are helping your earth by buying environmentally friendly products. You might not believe in it, but the smallest things can make a big change. By buying our environmentally friendly customizable jewelry, you are reducing the purchases of intoxicated and non-environmentally friendly products, which will slowly but surely make a difference in water life, wildlife, and our future.

Author Biography

My name is Vianca Santana, and I am 14 years old. I was born and raised in the Bronx, New York and I still live in the Bronx. My interests and hobbies are painting, listening to music, watching Netflix and baking. Listening to music makes me happy. I have a big family and I am the oldest out of the new generation. In my spare time, I like to take naps or listen to music. In the future I want to be famous.

Wilson's Bakery
Wilson Segarra

At Wilson's bakery we want everyone to get the taste of delicious food. We donate 10% of our bakery's income to charity. We make any dessert you can think of and custom birthday cakes. All of our products are hand made with local fresh ingredients.

We use local and fresh ingredients while donating to charities. While living in New York I have seen many homeless people who are trying to get their life on track but can't get help, so I wanted to be the one to help them. Baking was a hobby I had so I thought of how I could use it in a good way.

My business' mission is to help people in need of food. to help people in need of work. This is my business' mission because I see homeless people very often throughout New York. My business can be defined as a bakery. My business values hard workers and giving everyone a chance no matter where they are from. The cause I would like to support because of this are the homeless and POC. I chose to support this cause because POC are constantly discriminated against in the workforce. I chose to promote the principle of *No Discrimination* because I see a lot of discrimination daily and its good for business. Promoting this principle would help make sure my business is ethical because I would have diverse workers and be advertised better. I believe all people deserve a chance especially if they have a disadvantage based on something they can't control.

We will have our own bakery. My product will be sold at the bakery. This is the best way to reach my customers because it gives them the freedom of choice. My product will be advertised on Instagram and Tiktok. I chose these platforms because I can make short films of my product. Our social media is used to also promote the company value of no discrimination. This is done by posting our diverse workers and deserts.

We invite you to stop at our store at 11am - 5pm on Saturday to try our free samples. Remember, supporting us is supporting people in need.

Author Biography

I am Wilson Segarra. I am 15 years old, born and raised in the Bronx. I have been playing games for the majority of my life and have had an interest in baking for a couple of years. In the future, I want to run some sort of business like a bakery.

Fire Drawing.Co
Janniyah Strong

If you really want to show off your skills in drawing and still be safe but also have a lot of fun doing something you love, then you've come to the right place. Welcome to Fire Drawing. Here at Fire Drawing.co our business model is "Teaching others how to draw in a way we can't discover and know about yet." Slightly similar so people can have a way of developing their drawing skills and get out in the world and show what they can do. To do this I want to help others with something they are good at in life or a little activity to help out stress or boredom. Kids and adults today are actively bored and stressed out and their lack of hobbies after school is pretty much out of this world but with my business to help with that maybe things can go differently."

My business will teach people to not be afraid of their skills or about something that they are good at. They shouldn't have to hide their talent. By showing that it isn't that hard to show your skills in drawing, I will demonstrate my love for clip art style art and how to draw. Another way is that drawing helps with my emotions when I'm bored, upset or happy. This idea came to me because I want to show people that they shouldn't be scared about something they love to do or something they enjoy doing.

Our mission is to help people in their drawing skills to also better themselves in their fears if they have any. My business' mission is to make sure if anyone has a potential to draw and they're too afraid to embrace something they like to do, it's ok. My business can help with that. No one should be scared of something they enjoy. This is to bring something to life, to make like, let's say, another you, for example. This is my business' mission because I just want to help out and make people's lives a little bit easier to live. No one should have to be afraid of it. By defining my business, I see it as a way to help out and bring everyone's creation to life, and to not be scared. Not everything has to be perfect, 100%.

My business can be defined as a way to develop everyone's skills in drawing. My value in my business is to make sure that everyone gets their chance to show off what they can do so that one day they can help out others. The cause I would like to support because of this is Black Girls Code. As they say on their website, "Providing the African-American youth with the skills to occupy some of the 1.4 million computing job openings expected to be available in the U.S. by 2020." I chose to support this cause because a lot of people have the skills to make something of themselves and make a difference and help everyone.

I chose to promote the Fair Trade principle of No discrimination and gender equity because I value everyone, no matter the color of their skin or how well you do your job. Promoting this principle would help make sure my business is ethical because in this world everyone and anything has a job here, without discriminantion. With all due respect, this business will do their very best at helping everyone doing what they want with their skills.

Our placement. We prefer on weekdays to be online to keep things chill and safe and at a lovely park on the weekend. My product will be sold as a way of showing everyone to not be scared to try new things or something they're good at doing and can be sold online. This is the best way to reach my customers because due to what is happening in the world, it's a much safer and outgoing way to meet new people and best for people to just embrace what they have.

As a business we want to promote our business to platforms like Youtube, Instagram, and Tiktok to get more views faster and use hashtags to make everything work out the way it should. Overall, this is a good way of showing that the placement and promotion is that you can do anything all you need is a little help. Our social media is used to also promote the company value of bringing everyone together to make this in a way better and make everyone feel more comfortable. This is done by posting Hashtags, video references, and videos to teach others.

Fire Drawing.co invites you to show off your skills, by doing your very best at our studio. Feel free to share with your friends and family whoever you want, in order to support our company in any way you can. When you choose to support Fire Drawing.co you're not only choosing to help everyone around you, you are also choosing to help yourself. You can teach others to have the skills and never be afraid to open up.

Author Biography

My name is Janiyyah Strong. I am 15 years old. I was born Here in America. I was raised in Elizabeth, New Jersey. I like to sleep to have energy. I love making Tiktok to distract myself from any problem I have. The ones I love make me happy. My family is- well um different. In my spare time I want to feel motivated to do things so I mostly sleep or think I don't have any options for my future just yet. I do wanna go to college but I don't know what to be.

AnimeDezigns
Jeremy Ventura

AnimeDezigns aims to change the struggle women have to go through especially single mothers because one design at a time while encouraging no discrimination, gender equality, and equal pay and letting everyone know that employees should have equal pay despite gender or race.

Women for years have been struggling working double shifts then coming home and doing house chores and cooking. It's hard for them because I was raised by a single mother myself and when you see your mother cry from all the work she has to do it breaks you. That's why I'm going to make my business give women good pay and also free daycare while they work. My customizing company and what makes it unique is that we take designing to the next level with spray paint. We also have the best of the best taking their time with our product. My product is affordable for the community and first-time purchases get a free gift in their order.

An important fact about my business is that I'll try my best and do everything in my power to make sure none of my, co workers or employees get discriminated and Ill accomplish that by making zoom calls and putting all my workers in group and let them talk to each other on how they feel about what's happening in society and how WE as a business can change that little by little.

What makes my product special is that it's unique because, if you see anime, you see it in shows but this time you can have it on your clothing. I'm in love with anime. It inspired me to create a business based on it and I just want to bring other people in the anime world and show them how cool it is! AnimeDezigns represents me because I get to do designs and it helps me show my creativity and talent to others. We include all aspects of whatever anime you want. I was in class one day watching anime and I thought to myself "how cool would it be to have anime designs on clothing and wear it outside to "flex" and that's exactly what I was able to do with my business.

My business' mission is to Help Women financially, especially single mothers because I know how hard it can be. This is my business' mission because my mother inspired me to do this and I want to make her proud by helping women who are going through the same hell. a strong upholding company that promotes and also financially supports women. My business can be defined as an upholding company that promotes financial support for women and also makes them stronger .

My product will be sold both online and in stores. This is the best way to reach my customers because it's easier and I can also make videos and since everyone is quarantined more viewers will see my work. I will be promoting AnimeDezigns on YouTube because Facebook is not something I'm familiar with and also twitter is for posting short paragraphs I could use Instagram but i just find YouTube more convenient because i could post videos quickly and easily without issues. During my videos I'll try to merge the fact that I want to help single mothers.

Join us and do what's right and that's to help single mothers, Women in general and we need to show them respect and give them the same chances as everyone else. My company takes time to dedicate it into helping others. By supporting AnimeDezigns you're also supporting the cause .you'll be able to help those single mothers out there struggling.

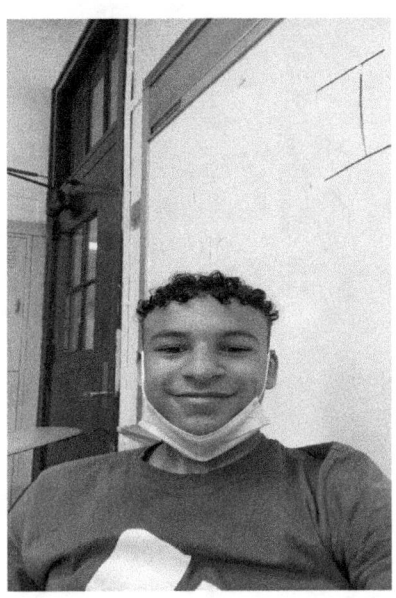

Author Biography

Hey, my name is Lucas and I'm 14, born in Manhattan, Washington Heights and raised in the Bronx. My hobbies are usually playing sports such as basketball and making anime designs. One thing that makes me happy is spending quality time with my family, and also making designs (mostly anime). In the future, I hope to become successful and make sure my mom doesn't work another day in her life. That's all I want for the future.

www.ingramcontent.com/pod-product-compliance
Lightning Source LLC
Chambersburg PA
CBHW072216170526
45158CB00002BA/622